Endorsements

"I am delighted to unreservedly endorse Carrie Ann Barrette's encouraging and instructive *Put Your Crown On*. Some authors write to fill pages, Carrie Ann writes to fill hearts."

—Gregory J. Austin, Th.D.
Author, *Shaken, Memoirs of A Life Lived in the Pursuit of Heaven's Heart*

"In this book, *Put Your Crown On*, Carrie Ann will eloquently inspire you on how to become all that God created you to be, and through His precious gift of salvation, you are called and destined to walk in Kingdom authority as Royalty to rule and reign over the earth! Are you ready to put your Crown on?"

—Sandra Benaglia
Founder, Apostle, Pastor, Fresh Fire Apostolic Ministries

"There are many Christians in America who do not understand what it means to have any kind of authority in Christ whatsoever. The New Testament Holy Ghost power has been zapped from American culture and thought of as a thing of past revivals. Carrie does an amazing job of not only debunking this with her own experiences with the manifestation of God's power, but also backing everything up with scripture. *Put Your Crown On* is an easy-to-read book that not only is a great study guide for new Christians, but also gives us a deep dive in what it really means to operate fully in the purpose God has for our lives. *Put Your Crown On* is a beacon of hope for not only New England, but for our entire nation."

—Lissette Carter
Author, Rookie AmeRican

"Carrie's book *Put Your Crown On* is a love story of a wonderful God who redeems us from our life's circumstances and restores us back to Himself. He then gives us His authority and lets us reign with Him as we help make the name of Jesus famous and fulfill the great commission. I love how the Lord is raising up both sons and daughters to have a voice in this generation and He is pouring His Holy Spirit out on both male and female! Exciting message for exciting times we are living in!"

—*Michael De Jong*
Founder of Zion International & Activation Church

"Jesus taught 'as one with authority.' You will be encouraged, inspired, and discipled to walk in the authority Christ has given you, as you read this book!"

—*Teresa DeMatos*
Pastor, Indian Lake Church

"This book will challenge you, stir you and fill you with Kingdom truths that when manifested through you will have the power to change the world! When we choose to walk in our God-given authority and gifting powered by Holy Spirit the world will see before them an unstoppable vast and mighty army. This book is a strategic guide to carrying out our roles as royals rightly wearing our crowns.

Well done Carrie Ann Barrette! You nailed it."

—*Darlene Curry*
Core Staff Leader at Redemption House Life Center, Fellow Author, and Artist

"The very thing that captures my heart about this amazing book, *Put your Crown On*, is its incredibly accurate sense of where we are in history and how we should be responding to the times. This book speaks volumes to how prophetically, God is calling forth sons to reign and rule as kings and priests."

—*Dr. Cadarrall A. Edding,*
Founder of Emerge Global Mandate, Inc.

"We live in a state of increasing fatherlessness. Society has lost sight of our awareness of the love God and parental authority is being abdicated for the latest cultural trends. This has plunged us into a widespread societal identity crisis that crosses cultures and lands. We live in a generation that is hungry for a loving Father to tell us who we are.

Carrie Ann Barrette skillfully guides us to rediscover our identity and destiny through Jesus. *Put Your Crown On* will take you on a practical and thoughtful journey that awakens you to the spirit of adoption (Romans 8:15) that firmly places you in a household of royalty with royal benefits but also royal responsibilities. Read on and enjoy the journey!"

—Paul David Guidry
Pastor, Bridge MetroWest

"Not only does *Put Your Crown* On lay solid Biblical foundations for this transition and this new day, but it also provides thought provoking questions and action steps that will make these principles specific and practical for you, wherever you find yourself on your spiritual journey."

—Virginia Killingsworth
Worship Leader, Minister,
Author, *Miracles Are Normal*

"In a day and age when identity is so confusing, to know who we are is vital! In this book, Carrie Ann answers that question. As you read this book you will see clearly your position and purpose in the kingdom of God. It will leave you empowered and free to walk in a blessed and beautiful relationship with your creator bringing heaven on earth."

—Kaeley McNeil
Writer, Humbly in Awe

"My favorite line in Carrie Ann's book is this: 'We are not who we believe we are. We are who GOD believes and says we are.' Knowing our true identity as sons and daughters of the King is essential in this hour. *Put Your Crown On* reminds believers that Kingdom rule and reign is done from a place of identity and authority IN CHRIST, who is above all!"

—*Deborah Perkins*
Founder, His Inscriptions

"I so appreciate Carrie Ann's heart throughout her book, *Put Your Crown On*. She helps the body of Christ discover who they are and Whose they are by putting their crown on and walking in the truth of the Word of God. She describes it as our "rightful place" within the Kingdom of God. Carrie Ann will help you identify and live within this Kingdom as you reign with The King."

—*Steve Prokopchak, MHS*
Author, *Identity: The Distinctiveness of You*

"Carrie takes the reader on a journey and compelling case that we ALL have a crown and unless you're wearing it with the eyes of understanding and knowing who you are in Christ, you're limiting yourself and the effects of demonstrating His insurmountable power. A new creation reality perspective with fresh conviction on the simplicity of the gospel for practicing without power for the whosoevers who choose."

—*Donna Scott*
Founder, Radiant Forge, Inc.

"Carrie Ann Barrette does a great job getting her readers to understand what their crown is and why wearing it is so important and it all goes back to our identity. Currently the whole world is struggling with their identity and of course this is foundational to knowing your purpose. Carrie Ann's heart and passion for the body of Christ to know Jesus and their identity in Him as stated in the New Testament of the Holy Bible is evident in her writing. Great read!"

—*Ann Wallace,*
Host, Divine Connections, Author, *Extraordinary Hope*

PUT YOUR CROWN ON

PUT YOUR CROWN ON

IT'S TIME TO REIGN LIKE THE ROYALTY YOU ARE

Carrie Ann Barrette

Put Your Crown On
Carrie Ann Barrette
www.liveoutlove.me

© Copyright 2023 Carrie Ann Barrette

All rights reserved.

This book is protected by the USA and International copyright laws. This book may not be copied or reprinted for commercial gain or profit. The use of short quotations or occasional page copying for personal, or group use, such as for Bible study, is permitted and encouraged by the author. Permission will be granted by request.

Cover design by Carrie Ann Barrette via Canva.com as per Canva's 2023 Canva Pro Content License Agreement available at:
www.canva.com/policies/contecnt-license-agreement
Crown by Alexroz. Background by IgOrZh from Getty Images

All Rights Reserved. No part (verbiage or artwork) of this book may be used or reproduced in any way without specific written permission by the author.

Scripture taken from the New King James Version®. Copyright © 1982 by Thomas Nelson. Used by permission. All rights reserved. Scripture taken from the Holy Bible, New International Version®, NIV® Copyright ©1973, 1978, 1984, 2011 by Biblica, Inc..® Used by permission. All rights reserved worldwide. Scripture taken from The Passion Translation®. Copyright © 2017 by BroadStreet Publishing® Group, LLC. Used by permission. All rights reserved. www.thePassionTranslation.com. Scripture taken from The Holy Bible, English Standard Version. ESV® Text Edition: 2016. Copyright © 2001 by Crossway Bibles, a publishing ministry of Good News Publishers.

ISBN: 9798868128585
Imprint: Independently published

Acknowledgements

Thank you, Lord, for sharing your heart and this message with me! It has been a blessing.

Thanks also to my best friend and husband Tim for faithful encouragement, a life of amazing partnership and lots of late-night editing! Tina and Krysti, thanks for praying me through this. Dad and Mom, you who taught me I was capable of bigger things than I thought and to never, ever stop learning. Thank you!

I also want to truly thank Dr. Pablo Polischuk for being unafraid to share stories of deliverance and spiritual warfare, which awakened me to the reality that the Holy Spirit still interacts with us today, John Sammons for sharing countless teachings on what the Lord was doing over about seven years, and Lee and Teresa DeMatos for pouring into our family as our pastors for ten years. God has used you all mightily!

Finally, Brian Hume, you have greatly spoken into my life and initiated this second round. Thank you. And Greg Austin, your kindness, encouragement, and prayers mustn't go unthanked.

Put Your Crown On

God is calling us to put our crowns on in recognition of His victory and our place in the Kingdom as His children!

Jesus paid to restore our role as children of God so we can reign in love and take back what the enemy has tried to steal. It is imperative that we take back our reign! Today, the world needs God's children to serve and lead more than ever.

Do you want to learn what it means to live out your supernatural destiny?

Put Your Crown On is a practical and easy to read overview of the rights and authority of the children of God as taught through His Word, with ten steps to help you learn how to rule, reign, and exercise the authority here on earth.

This will inspire you to put your crown on!

Put Your Crown On

1. In the Beginning 1
2. The Kingdom is at Hand 6
3. My Story 15
4. His Kingdom Looks Different 22
5. Coming Home 27
6. Who Are You? 39
7. In His Name 47
8. Warfare 60
9. Children Listen 72
10. Children Are Teachable 80
11. God Wants to Teach Us 85
12. Freedom for the Bride 92
Optional Prayer 102
13. Walking It Out 103
14. Ten Steps to Walking in Authority 111
15. Not Alone 121
16. His Children Teach 126
17. The Kingdom Is Love 133
18. Toss Your Crown 138
About the Author 143
Learn More 145

Foreword

There is a call from God, a Voice that resounds throughout heaven. It is a call to "*Put Your Crown On*." Carrie Ann Barrette, in this remarkable work, unveils a profound truth that has been embedded within the very core of our existence. God, in His infinite wisdom and boundless love, calls us to recognize our true identity as His beloved children, heirs to a Kingdom that knows no bounds. Through the redeeming sacrifice of Jesus Christ, we have been granted the extraordinary privilege of putting on the crown of authority, love, and purpose.

"*Put Your Crown On*" is a compelling testament to the unshakable victory that God has won on our behalf and the divine inheritance that is rightfully ours. It reminds us that we are not mere spectators in this grand narrative of creation but active participants. We are called to reign in love, grace, and truth, and to reclaim what the enemy has sought to steal from us. In these pages, you will embark on a journey of discovery, a journey that takes you through the profound and life-transforming truths of God's Word. Carrie Ann Barrette provides a practical and accessible guide, leading you through ten powerful steps to help you understand and exercise your authority as a child of God in the world today. It is an invitation to live out your supernatural destiny, a destiny that was designed before the foundation of the world.

"*Put Your Crown On*" is a clarion call to believers everywhere, reminding us that, in these trying times, the world needs God's children to rise, serve, and lead more than ever. Our faith is not passive; it is dynamic, alive, and world-changing. The time has come for us to grasp the depth of our identity and walk confidently in the power and authority that God has bestowed upon us. As you read this book, may you be inspired, encouraged, and equipped to put your crown on. May you rise to the challenge of living as a child of the King, with all the rights, privileges, and responsibilities that come with that honor. Through Carrie Ann Barrette's insightful guidance, you will be empowered to reign and to shine your light in a world that hungers for hope, love, and purpose.

So, my dear reader, embrace the call, heed the message, and *Put Your Crown On*. Your destiny awaits, and the world eagerly anticipates the radiant glory of God's children rising to fulfill their divine purpose. May your journey through these pages be a transformational experience, one that deepens your understanding of who you are in Christ and emboldens you to live out your calling. The time is now. The moment is here. Let us put our crowns on and take our place as heirs of the Kingdom. Next time I see you, I know you'll be wearing your crown!

Brian Simmons

Passion & Fire Ministries

A Note to the Reader

I have added scriptures related to the text. I have done so to encourage your study of the Word in relation to the subject matter. Please explore the Word in relation to what is written in this book. My goal is that this book might help guide you, the reader, towards Scripture's truth.

Additionally, this book is primarily about the truth for God's saved and born-again children, meaning those who have accepted Jesus as their Savior. Specifically, the adoption, deliverance, sanctification, authority, and power I have written about are all for God's children once they are saved by the blood of the Lamb, Jesus. All power and authority are endowed via the Holy Spirit, who is a gift to the children of God so we can reign rightly.

If you have yet to accept Jesus as Lord and/or have not asked the Holy Spirit to come be your helper, filling you with Himself, much of what I have written will not yet apply to your life, but it is offered to all of God's children. I pray you ask the Father to forgive you for the times you missed the mark and are led to ask Jesus to be your Lord, making His death on the cross your payment and trade for righteousness. May you follow Jesus in a process of sanctification, becoming like Him and ask the Holy Spirit to be your guide and helper in all things and to fill you with Himself. May the Father's rescue plan bring your rescue and deliverance, enabling the freedom and right relationship He desires with all His children.

Introduction

"Put Your Crown on!"

I heard the Lord speak these words to me in January of 2019. At first, I thought the words were just for me. Then I wondered if it was for my church, but soon I realized it was for everyone.

When I heard the Lord say, "Put your crown on", whether audibly or in my spirit, I didn't know; the words were strong and specific. Clearly, I needed to share these words with others. The Lord was asking me to help awaken His children to the reality of His Kingdom and their places in it.

As believers, we are sons and daughters of the Most High God with restored rights, authority, and roles in His Kingdom. This Kingdom is present and active now. He wants us to learn how to rule, reign, and exercise the authority Jesus won for us here on earth, taking the land and occupying until He comes[1] because:

"To live like this is all the more urgent, for time is running out and you know it is a strategic hour in human history. It is time for us to wake up! For our full salvation is nearer now than when we first believed." (The Passion Translation, Romans 13:11)

Today, God is calling us to awaken and put our crowns on in recognition of His victory and our authority as His children! He always intended for us to do so.

---

[1] Luke 19:13

The fall and sins of mankind hindered us initially, but because of Jesus' victory, we can now decide to step into our rightful and royal place under our heavenly Father[2] with the Holy Spirit's power, like our Brother Jesus.

Now we can take back our rights, authority, and identity as Children of God[3] which is what the enemy has tried to steal from the beginning.

The beginning… let's start there.

---

[2] Colossians 1:13 and 3:1, Ephesians 1:3-6 and 2:4-6

[3] Luke 19:13

Prologue

I have heard the story the book of Revelation conveys about saints casting their crowns before the King of Glory. I absolutely believe that will be the case. And in our hearts, it should always be the case before Him, even today.

But that time isn't now.

The here and now is the focus of this book. When I heard the Spirit say, "Put your crown on," I knew it was an imperative.

Now is the time to put your crown on!

In Scripture, the casting of crowns is noted like this: *"Around the throne were twenty-four thrones, and on the thrones I saw twenty-four elders sitting, clothed in white robes; and they had crowns of gold on their heads..."* (New International Version, Revelation 4:4) *"And they do not rest day or night, saying: 'Holy, holy, holy, Lord God Almighty, Who was and is and is to come!' 9 Whenever the living creatures give glory and honor and thanks to Him who sits on the throne, who lives forever and ever, 10 the twenty-four elders fall down before Him who sits on the throne and worship Him who lives forever and ever, and cast their crowns before the throne, saying: 11 'You are worthy, O Lord, To receive glory and honor and power; For You created all things, And by Your will they exist and were created'."* (New International Version, Revelation 4:8b-11)

Notice something...

THEY HAD THEIR CROWNS ON!!

Before they cast them down, they had them on. Like them, we need to put ours on before we can cast them down with an understanding of why His blood made us worthy of us doing so.

Some of you are reading that and saying, "Well, those are the twenty-four, and we are not them." Okay, maybe we are not them. I am neither Paul, nor one of the other twelve disciples. I am also not Mother Teresa, Heidi Baker, or Kathryn Kuhlman. However, like them, I am His child. Therefore, I am a princess, and if you are His, you are royalty too.

All children of the King wear crowns, figuratively or literally.

I encourage you to trust the word of God, that says all believers are His children. If you believe He is your redeemer and Lord, He is your Father.

You have a place in the Kingdom.

Royalty lives differently than others in the land. We can see that very clearly with British royalty. Even though their "power" isn't as it once was, their honor and stature are still intact. Royals act differently. They are treated differently by the people in the kingdom, but glory isn't the goal.

The goal of wearing a crown is to communicate authority, ushering in God's Kingdom, and will. When we understand who we are, we can then stand in our place in the Kingdom and play out our role. Understanding who we are is imperative. We cannot put on our crown and do so with authority if we don't believe this authority is available.

Believing in our identity is the key to the lock of the treasure chest containing our crowns. We are not who we believe we are. We are who *God* believes and says we are.

What's important is the way the King sees His children.

God sees us as His co-heirs with Christ.

Are you ready to learn how to put your crown on and reign with Him?

Study Questions

———————

1. Read Revelation 4:8b-11. In what ways do you feel like you are unworthy to wear a crown?

2. How might this be different if you were born into royalty?

3. God's Word says we are His children. If He deems you worthy of being a prince or princess, how does that change your concept of truth about your place in the Kingdom?

4. Read Daniel 7:27, Romans 8:16-17, and Ephesians 3:6. How do we, like princes and princesses, reign as co-heirs with our Heavenly Father?

1
In the Beginning

"Once upon a time in a land far away..."

This is how many stories start. They include a good king, a princess (or prince), and an evil villain who comes to ruin the plans of the king and sabotage his kingdom. It is not surprising that so many of our stories of old begin this way. A handsome prince comes to rescue the princess, and they live happily ever after.

In truth, this is how our story begins as well, right? Even in the Garden of Eden, there's a good King, His children, and Satan, the wicked, fallen one.

So, where is the happily ever after?

To some people, today looks much like the day before salvation. We may look at life and wonder where the Good News is. There is the hope of heaven, but that is an unknown time away.

What about today?

Indeed, our hearts desire a rescuer and a happy ending... change. We yearn, and hunger for it. Redemption is nestled in our core. In our hearts, we all cry out or search for a kingdom and for our rescue.

Because of this longing, we attempt to create and perfect a kingdom of our own. In the midst of the chaos of this world, we want to establish a place of controlled peace and happiness, removing or avoiding the pain of this world with a castle, including walls and a moat to protect us.

I did.

When I was in school, I worked to be valedictorian. Then, when out of school, I strived for years to become one of the "best" salespeople. I learned about business and then obtained a second degree so that I could work to set up my kingdom. I was told this was necessary for obtaining the 2.5 kids, house, spouse, and career which somehow would prove I had triumphantly achieved success, whatever that was.

Oh, I had such dreams about my kingdom!

Unfortunately, in my life, all this striving just led to fatigue, tears, and chaos.

The world around us is just that, isn't it? Tears and chaos.

Where is the good king? Our hero? Where is the prince who rescues us? Why are our clothes ragged and our bodies so weary of the toil?

Where is the joy? Where is the Good News?

We work so hard, yet we grow weary setting up our kingdoms. The success and peace we thought we would find as we built seems further and further away. It wasn't supposed to be like this. Was it?

No! Not at all!

There is a place like the one we search for.

It is a place of joy, rest, and peace… one with a good King. It is the Kingdom of God that we search for, and it is in our midst, but there is an enemy named Lucifer, who infiltrated the Garden of Eden and hindered us from remaining there. He is the fallen one who rose up in mutiny, defamed us and displaced us out of Eden.

Satan's goal is for us to believe God's Kingdom is a lie, and nothing will change that. He has always claimed God is a liar and His promises are moot.

Satan challenges, "Where is your rescuer?"

Those who heed his question and find no answer grow weary. This makes sense since the Bible says, "Hope deferred makes the heart sick." (New International Version, Proverbs 13:12) Many in the church are heartsick. Some believers have learned to maintain a level of hope, believing our King will return, but He has been so very long in His coming! We long to have our kingdom, our King, and our place in the Kingdom back. We long for the joy, peace, and place we once had and are told we will have.

But, when?

Generally, the church hangs onto salvation, believing, at least, in some future Kingdom. Though most Christians believe we have a righteous King and a Prince who ransomed us from death and judgment, much of the church believes we wait to see the Kingdom of heaven till we die, but no!

We don't have to wait. It is at hand NOW!

Jesus said, "The Kingdom is at hand," (New King James, Mark 1:15) but did He really mean today?

And what does that include?

The Kingdom of Heaven is available today, and it includes all He described in Scripture and all we have been longing for!

The book you are holding in your hands expounds on what Jesus taught in the Bible. I believe the Lord has been showing me and many others that the delay of the "ever after" of the Kingdom is really a lie from the pit of hell—from Lucifer himself!

Before I go on, know this. Right now, is like the moment in one of my favorite movies, called The Matrix wherein Morpheus sits with Neo. Like Morpheus, I am about to offer you two options. In one, you shake your head, close this book, and go back to building your own kingdom, while waiting for Jesus. However, if you keep reading, your eyes might be opened to the truth… and the truth can set you free![4]

---

[4] John 8:32

Study Questions

1. Like me, do you have any areas or experiences wherein you have felt God didn't seem to step in and you felt disappointed?

2. In what ways did you strive to build your own kingdom and watch it not match what you hoped? How is this different from the way Jesus says to build in Matthew 7:24-27 and 1 Corinthians 3:11-14? Also, how might Matthew 28:18-20 relate to Kingdom building?

3. John 8:44 notes Satan is the father of lies. What lies might Satan have told you about yourself and God that have led to a distance between you and the Lord?

4. Read Proverbs 13:12, which relates to feeling hopeless. How might it feel to be free and have hope again in light of Lamentations 3:21-23, Romans 5:1-11, and Romans 8?

2
The Kingdom Is at Hand

Once we have decided to accept the Lord as our Savior, the next step is to learn how to do life with that in mind.

What now?

How do we walk out our salvation and our new lives? How do we understand the Good News of the Kingdom and apply Jesus' teachings? And what is this Kingdom anyway?

The Kingdom of Heaven is the present reality of life with the Holy Spirit both here on earth and later in Heaven. It comes with freedom, victories, and authority. It comes with gifts of joy, love and a new family.

The Good News we talk about is not just that Jesus was born and died for us. It is why Jesus was born and died, and why the Holy Spirit came.

Yahweh, the King and Creator of the universe, has two goals:

- Reunite His Family (setting us in a relationship with each other and with Him).
- Reinstate His children into their places as co-rulers within the Kingdom of God.

He wants His children to live as they should have since the beginning. God's children were never meant to serve Satan. God was to be their Father, a good father.

As recorded in Genesis, God created a place for Adam

and Eve to bring forth life with Him; in a garden, a perfect place for them to do so. He said it was good. He was content. God enjoyed the humans and animals.

I think God had a ton of fun creating everything! I wish I could have been part of that, don't you? The stars, the seas, the animals… and two humans! Two perfect creations made in His image.

God called them good.

He called it all good.

God must have enjoyed it; after all, He walked with them in the cool of the day, and He fellowshipped with them. I imagine it was like a parent visiting his children. Maybe He asked them how they liked the animals, the stars, and each other.

God's children likely had a very intimate relationship with Him. Given that He was and is a kind and loving God, why wouldn't they have? I can see Him teaching them about the animals and the heavens, telling them how He created them all. That He created these things for them to enjoy.

God let Adam name all the creatures, even Eve. He put Adam and Eve in the garden to tend it, care for it, and enjoy it. Adam was told to go forth and multiply, filling the earth. He was told to subdue it.[5]

He was to reign with Eve and his family.

What an amazing Kingdom! I can get stuck there, pondering it all. Unfortunately, we know what seemed to be the original plan would not remain.

Suddenly, it was all taken away. That proud and fallen

---

5 Genesis 1:28

angel, Lucifer, wanted to be like God. Heck, he wanted to be God! He coveted the love the children had for their, as well as their relationship with and the admiration of the Father. Lucifer wanted to be admired, listened to and followed like God. He wanted our attention and worship. He would even risk losing his own place in the heavens to get it—to get us to follow him.

Known as Satan on earth, Lucifer carried out his plans. In part, he seemed to have succeeded. He was able to distract the children from their father, the prince and princess from their king. He was able to "kidnap" them from their Kingdom and seemingly destroy the King's family.

Though clothed with skins, Adam and Eve were sent out of the garden. In heeding the snake's advice, mankind had come under Satan's authority instead of the true King's. Because of this, Adam and Eve could no longer live in God's Kingdom while also following Satan's authority, nor could they serve a King they mistrusted.

By doubting the King's trustworthiness, Adam and Eve had given their authority and, in a way, their crown to the liar.

The righteous King, their Father, had to pronounce judgment and follow through with what might seem to many to be heartless punishment. Adam and Eve were no longer able to walk with their Father in the garden. They were banished so they would not eat of the tree of life, which would have caused them to live forever in judgment, separation, and fear. What an uncomfortable cliffhanger!

Many stories throughout the Old Testament note the Lord, our King, hinting at something more, something better... someday. The Old Testament promises the reunification of the line of Adam and Eve back into relationship with the King[6] and reestablishment of the Kingdom... but when? Where is our rescue?

Most of the promises and covenants point to God's desire to bless His children, to care for them, and lead them *if only* they are willing. With the weight of His children's shame so heavy and the lies so large, regaining what has been lost seems impossible. With each Old Testament story, the King reaches out, but His children turn away in fear, disbelief, or selfishness to false gods.

Do we still see God's care and guidance of His people in the Old Testament? Yes. Do we see victory and favor for His people? Yes, but the fullness of these promises seems far from fulfilled. Even when we look at the New Testament and the Promises of Jesus, do we really see all He promises fulfilled?

Yes!

It is in the New Testament, which focuses on the present-day restoration of the Kingdom.

It is the account of the hand of God reaching into this world and restoring the brokenness, restoring the relationship, and restoring His royal family. Looking back, we see that the King, our Father, never gives up!

Like a parent whose children have been stolen; like a prince whose bride is captured and wooed, the rescuer never stops! He will get His children back!

Hallelujah!

The idea of Christ as our rescuer brings to mind scenes from the movie *The Princess Bride*. In the movie, it seemed for a while that the farm boy named Westley loved the princess

---
6 1 Cor. 15:21, 22

quietly from a distance, responding only with the words *"As you wish"* and then disappearing, but in truth, that prince never gave up his pursuit for her no matter how *"inconceivable"* it seemed.[7]

No matter how inconceivable, like Westley, Jesus never gave up on us!

He will never give up on us!

I once had a similar vision during a time of worship at my church. The song playing was "Reckless Love,"[8] and my vision was of the Prince. He had jumped on the back of a horse that struck the ground mightily; hoof beat after hoof beat, as the Prince drove him and pressed down into his back at a gallop. He dug up the grass as he charged to the rescue of His beloved. I only saw the horse's hooves as they struck the ground hard again and again. There was no stopping Him in the vision, and indeed, there is no stopping Him now!

He won! He rescued us, and He is rescuing us.

The Good News is not only that He came, but that He is coming again! Part of the Good News is that the family line has also been put back in the correct order. God has redeemed and restored authority and relationship. The restoration of God's Kingdom has already begun. Many believers miss this part. It is what Satan wants us to miss entirely—that redemption and restoration are already accomplished.

As it is written, the baby born in a manger was Jesus, the promised Son who would take upon Himself the judgment due because of the sin of the world. Jesus was the promise

---

[7] The Princess Bride. Rob Reiner. Andrew Scheinman. Twentieth Century-Fox Film Corporation. (1987). Film.

[8] Asbury, Cory. "Reckless Love." Reckless Love (2018), via Bethel Music. Track 1.

born to Mary.[9] He was the one who would serve as a sacrifice for the sins of fallen, fearful, and disbelieving children.[10] His death would serve as payment to restore relationships and reinstate God's children. It would allow His children—God's prodigal sons and daughters—to come back into a right relationship with the Father as His heirs.[11]

He was our ransom.

Christ was the spotless Lamb found in a manger and sacrificed for the sins of the people, the blood payment due,[12] for the sin of all those willing to believe and desire reunification with the Father.

I don't know about you, of course, but I didn't know any of this as a kid—anything. Like some of you, I had to search this out and glean from others' understanding... and it took years!

I didn't understand the perfection and fullness of God's cleansing in my life. I thought I had to keep cleaning myself and apologizing, beating myself up as if His work was incomplete. I did not understand the fullness of forgiveness and the right standing I had in the Father's eyes because of Jesus.

Yet even in my ignorance, I was completely restored as His beloved child, reinstated as a co-heir and co-ruler with Jesus in the Kingdom, as Adam and Eve were originally created to be.

---

[9] Luke 24:27

[10] John 3:16

[11] Luke 15: 11-32

[12] Genesis 3:21, 22:1-19, Leviticus 1711, Hebrews 9:22, 1 Peter 1:19

These are the things I feel the Lord has been showing me more and more in the last few years. He wants me to understand; he wants you to understand the fullness of what the Son and the Father did through Jesus for us.

He made a way in the darkness and chaos.

The rescue plan commenced and was fulfilled. It is no fairytale. *"It is finished."* (John 19:30, NIV)

The payment is complete for everything!

It was COMPLETE!

We must believe this part, that there was nothing left to be paid or righted, nothing left undone.

We not only need to believe it was full payment, but we *also* have to believe there was a payment due and then accept that HIS payment covered what was due and restored us. If we do not, His death and resurrection is a foolish act with no reward.

Maybe the Lord would have been right to call down His angels and wash His hands of us. Instead, He is gracious, slow to anger, and forgiving. To some, it might seem a waste for Him to suffer for children who would never accept His payment for them, but He was willing to die for *everyone* because He wants everyone to be redeemed.

He wants you free and restored.

As I noted, I did not understand this when I was young. I hadn't a clue. I just saw the brokenness of the world and the hopelessness. I did not know hope. Truth brings hope.

Study Questions

1. Read Matthew 4:17, Matthew 6:10, and Colossians 1:13. What is the Kingdom of Heaven to be like?

2. The word says the Lord is a place of refuge or safety. Read Psalm 18:30.

3. Isaiah 26:3-4, Psalm 9:10, and Proverbs 3:5-6. In what ways do you sometimes doubt His trustworthiness? How does this contrast to His word?

4. What are some ways a lack of healthy relationships with your earthly father might hinder your view of the Lord as a perfect Father?

5. Romans 8:14-17 notes that we have the spirit of adoption when we cry, "Abba Father." What might it be like to be fully rescued, adopted, and restored as a child of a perfect and loving Father?

3
My Story

When I was first told about the Good News, I saw a glimmer of hope and grabbed on with both hands. I was thirteen years old. At the time, I had watched one too many Nostradamus predictions. Even one is too many, but either way, between my parents' divorce and my mother's unhealthy second marriage, along with the fear of nuclear war (and yes, a few horror movies), I had been frightened into a state where I could barely sleep.

Then I went to a séance. Such meetings are obviously satanic rituals and, in no way, healthy. I didn't understand the truth of that, or the importance of avoiding them. I have repented for partaking in the event, but for me, there were good things that came about. How that could be possible is only by God's grace, but this is a significant part of my salvation story because God showed up.

Here's what happened...

At the séance, things started to happen that seemed supernatural. At one point, I thought I saw a being standing in a doorway, and a radio began to play when no one seemed to touch it. Let's just say things got weird. A young man there had thought to get a Bible. I had never held one or read one before. Thankfully, he found one there and opened it. With what you might call "Bible roulette," he landed on the phrase, *"The Lord rebuke you, Satan!"* (New King James, Zechariah 3:2)

Once this verse was stated, peace came.

Everything changed.

The sudden peace that came into the room was palpable. It seemed to consume everything else that had been there a moment before, as if someone had turned on a light and scattered the darkness. I was glad, but unsettled and confused. Though it was peace, it was so strong, sudden, and powerful, it scared me. I was undone! Who or what was so powerful that it could stop the spirits of darkness?

Who was this Lord that could rebuke the darkness?

I had a new type of fear in the midst of that peace. I feared and revered whatever brought the peace, for it was more powerful than the darkness.

I feared the Lord.

The problem now was that I didn't know this Lord, and I still was not sleeping at night.

At this point, my mother was afraid for me. She had no idea what to say to me in order to explain the experience or eliminate the fears I wrestled with. She didn't know how to help me to sleep either.

Because of this, and by God's grace, she asked a pastor (a business acquaintance of my stepfather) for help. I am so thankful she asked!

The pastor sat with us and shared about our need for forgiveness. He taught that if I could accept that Jesus died for me, I would be pronounced "not guilty" and would go to heaven when I died. However, I could not just know this truth. I had to accept it. I had to make it *my* truth.

I was completely willing!

I call that my *"ticket to heaven."* At that age and time in my life, all I really wanted was to not die and go to hell, so I was up for whatever made that true. The problem was that no one discipled me or taught me anything more. I went on with my teenage life with that "ticket" secure in my back pocket, but I didn't know my Savior. I didn't even know it was possible to know Him.

I have found that many people have similar stories. They might say the sinner's prayer at the altar, but they go home wondering what happens next.

Sadly, we often don't know there is more. There is much more!

To finish my story, I walked through the next ten years like anyone else. I lived like someone outside God's Kingdom.

I didn't know there was a Kingdom available to me.

Later, I read some of the Bible but was still focused on trying to build and secure my own kingdom while I wandered in the darkness, following others who stumbled around trying to find their own way. I tried to build my house and find my prince, but instead, my own kingdom was a mess. With much too much stumbling, I found myself broken and heartsick. I found myself and my soul downcast. What was it all for? What good did a ticket to heaven do for me now?

Hopelessness and self-disgust nearly overtook me.

One night as I stood in my apartment hall, one more heartache and disappointment down, I looked at the bathtub.

Plans came to mind to "fix" everything in one final action. In this one moment, a moment Satan meant for His own good, I gained what Satan never wanted me to know: my Savior. How? As I stood there, fearing the very thing that might bring an end to my suffering, I remembered a name.

HIS name.

There was something about His name.

In a puddle of tears, I called out to Jesus. I had no idea what that would do, but it seemed like my last hope. He was, in fact, my only hope. And at that moment, He came into the room. I encountered His presence and His peace, but this time with power *and* love.

Everything would be changed forever!

He was in the room!

He came and surrounded me in the Spirit. This is the best way for me to describe it. He came and surrounded me like a hug. My whole being knew who He was, and that He was there.

He encountered me.

He asked me a question. It was THE question.

"Are you willing to follow me?"

I believe this is the question He asks us all. Are we willing to follow Him?

I knew exactly what He meant. He wanted me to seek after Him, learn His ways, and do what He asked. I also understood He was kind. Previously, I hadn't had any idea my Savior was kind. His presence showed me so much kindness and forgiveness. He didn't judge me. It was an, *"I forgive you, now go and sin no more"* (New International Version, John 8:1) kind of message, except He didn't want me to go. I would later learn He wanted to walk with me in the cool of the day, *every* day.

He wanted a right relationship with me, His daughter.

Me!

For ten years, I was "saved" with my ticket to heaven in hand, but I had no idea God was in pursuit of my affection.

I was completely unaware!

It is so amazing that God wants a right relationship with all His sons and daughters. He wants to fellowship with all His children, and to reinstate His family, but He also wants to put them back into their rightful place in His kingdom. I still didn't understand this part for nearly another ten years.

I didn't know I had a rightful place in a Kingdom.

Since that encounter, I have been seeking to follow Him, my Lord, and my King. I know He is real. I know He is mine, and I am his. He has pursued me in a love affair that takes my breath away. However, I needed to be reprogrammed from all the world's teachings.

I had to learn that the enemy in the séance was real and that I was still connected to him in more ways than I understood.

The Lord is still showing me the depth and breadth of this and His Kingdom.

For those of you who have yet to encounter God in this way or know the depth of His love, know that it is possible to begin to right now. You too can call out to Him and ask that He reveal Himself and His ways: His love, His salvation, and His kingdom to you. Now can be that time. Put this book down and cry out to Him. He is ready to connect with you even more than what you have seen or understood. Because He loves you, this is His heart's cry too.

Salvation through forgiveness isn't the end of the story.

Salvation is only the commencement of your reunification. It is just the beginning of a mind change or awakening (repentance), the beginning of your reinstatement into the Kingdom.

This is the rest of the "Good News!"

We can all learn what it means to be children in the Kingdom of the Most High, learning about the good and true King, learning that there is a Kingdom *and* that there is a role for His children *in* that Kingdom.

We all have a place in the Kingdom! He will show you yours; just ask and follow Him.

Oh, there is so much truth available that can set us free!

What a crime that so many of us stopped at obtaining our ticket, so get your ticket as I shout, "Now boarding flight 101 to the Kingdom of Heaven!"

Study Questions

---

5. In what ways has your relationship with Jesus helped you cope with life and be ready for death?

6. Reading Matthew 4:19, what might it mean for you to follow Him?

7. Read Psalm 136:3, Galatians 4:6-7, 1 John 3:1, and Revelation 1:5. What might it mean to have a healthy relationship with the King of Kings as your Father?

8. The Good News is found in Luke 4:18 and 1 Peter 1:13-25. After reading these verses, describe the Good News and note what it means to you.

4
The Kingdom Looks Different

While I didn't know about the Kingdom, John the Baptist was waiting in the desert for the Kingdom. He knew the Kingdom of Heaven was coming. He was trying to proclaim its coming even before he was born, but how would He know when it came? He knew there would be a Christ and that this Christ would change everything. Even after John baptized Jesus and had heard of His miracles and teaching, he still asked Jesus if He was the Christ or if Israel should keep waiting.

The Jewish people had been waiting for their rescuer just like we have been. The Jewish people had always been looking for a rescuer. They believed someday God would fulfill His promises and would send the Christ, who would re-establish the Kingdom and their place in it. The problem was that they were and still are looking for another because Jesus didn't seem to fit the role they had assumed He would. They wanted another earthly king who would overthrow the Romans and put them in charge. They weren't looking for the Kingdom Jesus described; in fact, to them, it seemed a bit backwards. He was a shepherd boy after all.

This Jesus didn't seem like what they were looking for.

Jesus modeled and spoke of humble leaders who served

others, even the poor and prostitutes. The Jewish leader's view of a kingdom didn't line up with this sort of teaching on humility. Christ's perspective seemed foolish and beneath them.

The Jewish paradigm also didn't allow for the grace and mercy Jesus had for poor and downtrodden sinners who actually testified of who He was and what His Kingdom was like. Jesus' answer to John the Baptist was, *"Go and tell John the things which you hear and see: "The blind see and the lame walk; the lepers are cleansed and the deaf hear, the dead are raised up and the poor have the gospel preached to them. "And blessed is he who is not offended because of Me."* (New International Version, Matthew 11:4-6)

Jesus was walking out the example of a different King and a different Kingdom than they were expecting. It was much, much better and it was present tense, but it did offend the Jewish leaders.

When Jesus began teaching, *"Repent, for the kingdom of heaven is near,"* (New International Version, Matthew 4:17) the Kingdom of God was right before their eyes, and so was their Prince.

They didn't see that their Rescuer had come.

They didn't see any Kingdom—not in what Jesus was describing.

They had no concept of a Kingdom consisting of permanent payment for sin, love and acceptance, or reinstatement into a spiritual family.

Everything they were waiting for was standing before them in humility.

Humility wasn't what they wanted. They were looking

for another David or Solomon to sit on an earthly throne and reign there forever, fulfilling the role of the promised anointed king with power and judgment. They were awaiting a hostile takeover or a coup d'état.

Meanwhile, the God of Abraham, Isaac, and Jacob continually attempted to paint a different picture for them. He would overthrow the enemy while proving Himself their guardian, provider, warrior, and rescuer again and again. He would do this as their Father, not as an iron-fisted king from the earth, in the way they desired.

God was about to fulfill the plan He made in the beginning.

If you tie all the stories in Scripture together and look at the Lord's countless offers of covenant blessings, you end up with the very love story and Kingdom we have all been searching for. God the Father wanted to be their helper, guide, and caretaker. Throughout Scripture there is story after story of His glory.

His glory is the testimony of His kindness and blessing.

The prodigal son story in Luke fifteen is one of the more descriptive stories of the Lord's love for His people. It was for the Jews, but also for all mankind. The son didn't want to be under the king (his father). He was determined he could make it on his own. He attempted to be his own ruler and failed miserably.

Sound familiar? It does to me.

Only when he reached the end of himself did he go back to his father with a changed mind. That is me. That might be you.

And what about the King?

The Father?

He threw a party, even sacrificing the fatted calf and putting a ring on his finger! The relationship and his son's role in the Kingdom were made right.

The father rejoiced in the son's return to the Kingdom!

He could reinstate him and once again serve and protect his son, teach him, and spend time with him. Do you hear His heart? He is waiting for us to come back under His headship and be part of His Kingdom.

God's heart is restoration.

He is always reaching out His hand. The Kingdom is still all around us. If we can believe it and see everything through the eyes of the Kingdom, then, and only then can we walk in that love. No matter where you have been or what you have done, He wants you back. We are the missing piece of His puzzle. *"Which is the most important piece? The missing one..."*[13]

You.

You have a place in His Kingdom!

We all do.

---

[13] Ron Myer, Assistant International Director- Dove International. Quoted from a sermon given at Indian Lake Church, Worcester, MA.

Study Questions

1. Ephesians 1:5 notes we are adopted into His family through Jesus. In what ways might it seem too good to be true that God might welcome you into His family?

2. In Matthew 4:17, Jesus speaks of repentance. What does repent mean per 2 Chronicles 7:14, Mark 1:15, and Joel 2:13?

3. Read Luke 15:11-32. How could changing your mind about Him and how He sees you change your life?

4. A covenant of blessing is found in Deuteronomy 28:2-11. Others are found in Isaiah 59:21, Jeremiah 32:40 and Hebrews 9:15. What do these show about His nature and care as we trust Him and join His family in a covenant of blessing through Jesus?

5
Coming Home

God's desire has always been restoration.

His will is that all the problems that created division between Him and His children in the beginning, and still do, be done away with. He desires and sets forth a plan so that we and everything we lost is restored.

What stands in our way now? Surprisingly, not Him.

We do.

Each of us can stand in the way of being in right relationship with our Father, the marvelous King and walking out restored sonship and authority.

How?

If we haven't heard the Good News or we don't believe we need Him, we won't be looking for Him or see Him. Our eyes and minds will be closed to Him, and we will miss out on the truth that can reveal our future. Because of this, we won't reach out for Him in desperation or humbly trade our lives for His.

When I was young, I never knew God. I might have heard His name, but it was not said in honor. I did not go to church except once on Easter. All I knew was that church was cold and uncomfortable. I did not feel involved or at ease.

As I grew up, I had no understanding of what a Bible was. I knew that it was a holy book of some sort, but I had no concept of what "holy" meant. The only right and wrong I felt was determined by my family's culture and teaching. I had a grandmother who said most people were stupid and made bad choices. This led me to attempt to search out and make good choices, whatever those were.

When I was older, I began to hear more about God and Jesus, but I had no understanding of my lack. I did not know I needed Him. I had no concept of His impact on my life except that He was supposedly the Son of God and that he opposed Satan. Strangely, I always believed Satan existed. I knew I didn't want to run into him.

This whole time; however, I had no concept of the goodness of the Good News, what God did for me, or how He loves me. A heavenly family wasn't a concept I understood. I didn't know what depravity was, nor that I suffered from it. My mind did not know or desire repentance except when I made a choice I didn't like. I wasn't humble or desperate for God yet. I was ignorant, but I didn't care.

I needed an experience that led me to awareness of truth and *my* need for Him.

This experience is crucial.

To gain any entry or rights to His family or to the Kingdom, we must take these steps:

1. Accept our need for Him and His bloodshed as the payment for our sin. For this to happen, we need repentance which is our change of mind. We change our minds, recognizing our sins against God and His creation as well as our need for His "covering" or debt payment.
2. Apply the payment. Our debt must be paid by His blood, the only acceptable payment.[14] We need to accept Christ's Body, broken for ours, as the payment for our *shalom*:

---
[14] Hebrews 9:22

peace, prosperity, and health.
3. Accept His resurrection for ours. We are reinstated into Kingdom authority, and then are we re-seated with Christ in heavenly places.

This last step is often missing. We must accept the payment due to return to our place in the Kingdom and our reign.

In Christ, we are now rulers on the earth, and at the same time, we are reigning and ruling in heaven with Him. Our authority is already complete here, and we don't have to wait until we get there.

Have you ever heard that not only was our sin payment fulfilled, but our authority was also completely restored? I really hadn't. I didn't know anything about spiritual authority, but it is in the text. Ephesians 2:6 reads, *"He raised us up with Christ the exalted One, and we ascended with him into the glorious perfection and authority of the heavenly realm, for we are now co-seated as one with Christ!* (The Passion Translation, Ephesians 2:6)

Furthermore, in Romans 8, the Scriptures read, *"And since we are his true children, we qualify to share all his treasures, for indeed, we are heirs of God himself. And since we are joined to Christ, we also inherit all that he is and all that he has. We will experience being co-glorified with him provided that we accept his sufferings as our own."* (The Passion Translation, Romans 8:17)

This is why Jesus came, suffered, and died to restore (Family and His heirs).

He wants us to inherit ALL He is and has.

ALL.

When I was writing this, I came across a well-written

nugget of truth from a writer I hadn't heard of in a small church in Minnesota. I didn't know him or his teachings, but these words were concise:

"When Jesus died, we died with Him. When He rose from the dead, we rose with Him. When we receive Jesus as Lord of our lives, all that He did belongs to us! What He accomplished, He accomplished for us. In the mind of God, we are included in all that he did. When Jesus came out of the grave, you came with Him. You no longer need to live under the condemnation of death, but you can rise in newness of life."[15]

And what is this newness of Life?

It is life in the Kingdom.

Is this trade worth it? There is nothing worth more. That is why He traded.

All of Him for me.

All of Himself for you.

All of the Son for all the Father's lost children.

To what end? Just so that we could go lie on fluffy clouds and play harps? Isn't that what the end is?

No! Hear me! Goodness no!

Sadly, this is the belief of so many. Their ticket to heaven ends with harps, clouds, and little cherubs. Listen, I make no fun. I was there. I thought that for decades but, the Kingdom is now! And the Kingdom is so much more than I understood!

It is not just the heavens that we can look forward to.

Heaven is surely amazing, and I await the time that I

---

[15] Shanklin, Tom, and Tom and Susan Shanklin. "Welcome to Tom Shanklin Ministries!" *Tom Shanklin Ministries*, Tom Shanklin Ministries, 20 April, 2020, www.shanklinministries.org/.

might see it fully with my own eyes instead of with spiritual eyes or in my mind, but that is not the only benefit from the "trade" of our lives. Of course, I look forward to seeing the room He made for me, to seeing the intricate handiwork and beauty of heaven, and to seeing the Lord, the One my heart longs for.

Yet what is this spiritual place we are in, called the Kingdom of God? How do we live in it? Engage it? Participate in it now?

Where is it?

The reality of the Kingdom is actually so much like the fairytales of old; it seems too good to be true. Let me explain.

The Kingdom of heaven is here presently.

It is around you right now. We don't have to wait for it. It is not *in heaven*, but *of heaven*. In fact, it is here on this earth. The Kingdom of heaven is all around us. Most of us don't see it, and few perceive it, but it is here as promised. We might have some idea of heaven's reality. Generally, we believe angels and demons roam the earth. Most people aren't really sure why or what they are doing, but do have some concept of their reality. Perhaps, as I did, they even believe in Satan.

All these creatures are real. They were created by the LORD. With regard to the Kingdom; however, there is one more being who makes the Kingdom of heaven possible. More than all the heavenly creatures, with you even now is the Holy Spirit, our Comforter.[16]

That might be enough to jump in on the trade of our life for His, but most don't know the Holy Spirit even exists, never mind that He is active in our lives.

---

[16] John 15:26 and 16:7

The trade, our life for His… with a bonus!

When we accept Jesus as our Savior and enter into the covenant of blood offered by the LORD, we get a relationship with all three parts of the Trinity. We find a heavenly Father; a Brother and Husband; and a Comforter, and Helper. Each member of the Trinity offers an intimate relationship, one of guidance, protection, and provision.

The Holy Spirit is the helper.

The kindness and love of the Holy Spirit could be proclaimed endlessly. His presence, however, is often overlooked or misunderstood. Generally speaking, when He is perceived, the experience is so different from the norm that it is dispelled as an odd spiritual occurrence instead of one that is possible every day.

Even the first time he was seen after the Lord rose from the dead, He wasn't what anyone expected.[17] Not only this, but the Comforter brought things they had never seen!

Tongues of fire.[18]

New languages.

Power to heal, deliver, and even raise the dead!

These people did not know what was going on, but there was the Holy Spirit, the promised Helper moving upon them in surreal and supernatural ways. He came on them in power.

Why, though? What was this Helper for?

The Helper was set in place to fortify the Children in the Kingdom. The Holy Spirit assists and empowers them all

[17] Acts 1

[18] Acts 2

through life by guiding them into all truth, strengthening them when they are weary, and leading them to enforce their true victory through Jesus. He does this by helping and training them to stand in the truth of their sonship and their authority, which Jesus won back for them through His death.

The first believers needed power. As we do today, they had forces working against them, which they needed to overcome. The Helper came to help them rule. He came to help you rule with Him.

Rule with Him? Yes!!

He didn't come just to make you feel warm and fuzzy; telling you everything will be okay. Remember when I wrote about the Good King and the Kingdom? Well, it's a bit like the story of Robin Hood. The King is away. In this case, He is in heaven, but in either case, someone has to rule while He is away.

Yes, we are to rule with Him. Of course, we are to serve Him and others, but we also are to rule with Him in the Kingdom.

Ever hear of co-heirs? The Bible says we are *"joint heirs with Christ"* (New King James Version, Romans 8:17)…

Joint.

As in marriage.

This co-ruling is unsettling, maybe even hard to accept for many. How can the disciples rule and reign beside Jesus, who is perfect? We know that we and all humans are imperfect. Isn't there a risk to us ruling? People haven't done the best job thus far.

There is a part of us that knows that we who rule are imperfect. Imperfect governing is hard to watch, and sometimes needs correction.

Most of us want to be helpful and attempt to bring love and change, but our humanity and history of partnering with sin can get in the way of perfection. We know there is selfishness and corruption, just as there was in the story of Robin Hood. This righteousness is the struggle His children have in walking out their authority and His will in the Kingdom. Yes, maybe the Kingdom has been overtaken and the good King seems to be away, but He set us as caretakers.

God's imperfect children must, in their newfound identity, stand up and overthrow the enemy.

God knew of our inclination to sin ahead of time. For this reason, He designed His plan, even accounting for sin. His fully redeemed and cleansed Church (the children of God) is to die to itself in devotion and humbly walk in faith. When they do, they can advance and take dominion, ruling with authority in the Kingdom today.

Paul's and Peter's lives are examples to explore. Their lives, like Christ's, were just that—examples. They were imperfect, but the King wants us to follow Him, learn from Him and rule like Him.

And He will teach us, walk with us and help us.

The Holy Spirit is willing to actively participate and train us to reign.

Like Mr. Miyagi in The Karate Kid, we don't always understand the Holy Spirit or His ways, but He is wise and has our good in mind. He wants to prepare, train, and help us to reign in victory.

God always meant for us to rule.

Adam and Eve reigned in the garden. That was God's

design. They were to be a prince and princess, ruling and reigning with Him over the earth, advancing the Kingdom.

God's goal is the same now as it was in Eden. Like Adam and Eve, we are to go forth and multiply, not just in number, but in positional reign as children with authority exercising our dominion and rule. We are to take our seats (here, figuratively in authority on earth and there, spiritually in heaven) by His side and take up our place ruling the world in love and humility like our elder Brother *"for we are now co-seated as one with Christ!"* (The Passion Translation, Ephesians 2:6)

Psalm 8 is clear on mankind's authority noting, *"You have made them a little lower than the angels and crowned them with glory and honor. You made them rulers over the works of your hands; you put everything under their feet: all flocks and herds, and the animals of the wild, the birds in the sky, and the fish in the sea, all that swim the paths of the seas. LORD, our Lord, how majestic is your name in all the earth!"* (New International Version, Psalm 8:5-9) The problem is the same as it always was: Lucifer. Even now, this liar is completely bent on making sure we have no idea that authority or reign is possible. He wants us to doubt it, even fear it. On earth as Satan, he "reigns," but this isn't God's plan. It never was.

Who is supposed to reign?

You.

Me.

The struggling believer next to you at church and the strung-out homeless person who can't get his act together, but loves the Lord?

Yes, even them.

The Good King wants all his children redeemed, clean, restored, and reigning well at His hand.

Now, maybe you are pondering how in the world *you* can reign.

Maybe you are looking at the mess you have made thus far. I was. I was looking at my history.

He wasn't. He isn't.

He is looking at you with Him. It's new math.

(You − Sin) + Holy Spirit = Jesus.

Picture this just for the fun of it: all God's children using their God-given gifts and talents to help each other. All children laying down their old lives and picking up their new ones. These sons and daughters standing in faith, moving the mountains of sickness and disease, declaring freedom for the captives, and raising the dead—all His children serving one another, forgiving, binding demons and loosing the peace of God… all children asking the Lord what He thinks is best and doing things His way.

Now *that* would be different!

We have a picture of this in Acts, an example of the Kingdom.

Is this some socialist agenda? Nope. Not in the least. It is a Kingdom agenda, His agenda. It is an agenda for *shalom*. An everlasting peace and contented joy.

Maybe we won't get there untill the new earth, but we could try. God is asking us to try.

He is calling us to lean into Him and His word, listen to the Spirit, and walk in what He designed. We are to carry out His plans like Sons or Daughters.

We become the children we were designed, redeemed, and called to be one day at a time as we partner with the Holy Spirit and learn what might be possible.

We learn that there is a crown of glory that He has destined for us. Yes, there is a time and place to cast it down, but that time isn't now.

It's time to put your crown on!

Study Questions

1. Read Romans 8:15-34. What might be in the way of being in right relationship with your heavenly Father?

2. What have you understood about the Kingdom of Heaven being here presently? How can you participate in it, as in Matthew 16-19, and Revelation 5:10?

3. Acts 2:38 notes that believers received the gift of the Holy Spirit at Pentecost. Like them, how will the Spirit help us to serve and reign with the Lord, considering Isaiah 11:2, John 14:26, and Romans 8:26?

4. Read Acts 1:8, 1 John 5:2-3, and Revelation 5:10. What could it mean and look like for you to reign in this life as a child of God?

6
Who Are You?

If someone were to ask, "Who are you?" what would you say? Would you choose to share certain parts of your story? Might you share your accomplishments or experiences?

Would you describe the "you" of earlier, innocent years? Would it be you when you had great success or times you made terrible choices? Would you repeat what others said about you? Would you hide what you think because you don't like it?

Early on, I would often start my story with my parents' divorce and end with my life's regrets. Later in life, I would share my job title, noting that I was a salesperson or a mental health counselor, but maybe exclude my mistakes. I would convey who I was based on experiences, accomplishments, or failures.

Whatever you or I might share, that isn't who God says we are.

In Christ, you are a new creation.

The old is gone away, and the new has come.[19] I am a child of God and so are you.

Throughout this book so far, perhaps doubt or guilt has come across the screen or the airwaves in your mind. That is from the enemy.

---

[19] 2 Corinthians 5:17

Satan has always had one mission: to make God's children doubt their identity. He wants all humanity to believe they are unworthy of the Kingdom and unworthy to be God's children.

When we consider the Kingdom, our King's goodness, our place in the Kingdom, and our authority to act on His behalf, we must believe. If we do not believe, we will not act, and our potential in the Kingdom will be unmet. Maybe this is why Jesus teaches so often about faith. He even seems to get frustrated, saying, *"Oh you of little faith..."*. (New King James, Mt. 14:31)

Again and again, He teaches that we must have faith in Him and in ourselves in light of Him—what He taught and what He believes about our capabilities and place in the Kingdom.

God believes in us!

What's counterintuitive is that the enemy already believes in us too. In fact, Scripture notes, *"You believe that there is one God. You do well. Even the demons believe -- and tremble!"* (New King James, James 2:19)

Satan believes.

The demons believe—and notice that they 'tremble!'

The enemy believes not only in God, but also in the children's authority, and he obeys when they stand in faith on what their Father taught them.

Satan has been fighting against the rule of the King's children since the beginning. He doesn't fight against God. He fights against us, knowing our track record. He also fights because he knows we are the last piece of the puzzle. If the children understand their place in the Kingdom; if they walk in their authority, *really* walk in the victory won, Satan will no longer reign. He is defeated already. Satan just doesn't want us to believe it.

Will it be easy to maintain our faith right out of the gate? Will we stand firm in believing we are who God says we are? Maybe, but it is a fight. For one thing, the enemy lies and is stubborn, testing our authority. For another, sickness remains because of limited faith.

People ask, *"Why hasn't God acted?"*

He has!

The King taught His children and gave them authority and direction. He empowered them, gave them authority, and gave them a tutor to assist them against every question or foe. The authority doesn't make the enemy go away, but it equips God's children to defeat him.

Satan lingered to tempt Jesus. He will linger with us, too, until we stand in authority doing what Jesus did: fighting him with the truth of the Father's words about ourselves. Each time Satan tempted Jesus, he came with that same *"Did God really say?"* (New International Version, Genesis 3:1) argument.

Did God really say…?

This is the same line he always uses, but what did the Son do?

Jesus didn't cower.

He did not question or doubt who God was. He didn't question who He was. Each time Satan challenged Him; Jesus declared and stood on God's Word. He drew His spiritual sword and reminded Satan of what the LORD said. He kept right on believing in His Father's goodness. He kept completing God's plans. He kept standing in faith regarding His authority and Sonship. He knew who He was. This was the example He left for us. Our Big Brother was trained well!

If Satan can maintain the lie of mankind's unworthiness, he can maintain his "rule and reign."

Satan wants to reign.

If instead God's children awaken to their worth and to the truth, they can then overthrow Satan... and they inevitably will.

Spoiler alert: We win!

Scripture noted this victory in the very beginning. In Genesis 3:15 it is written that the seed of Eve will crush Satan's head.

He has! Now we can walk in Christ's victory.

We walk in victory when we stand in Christ's truth and overcome Satan's lie. This lie is the same as it has been from the beginning... "Who do *you* think you are?"

Satan tempted Jesus to doubt His identity, asking Him, *"If you are the Son of God..."* (New International Version, Matthew 4) Satan is famous for asking *"if"* or *"what if"* questions.

What if God isn't good?

What if He is a liar?

What if God doesn't love you?

What if you are not worthy?

These are the basic questions that hinder faith and keep us from our thrones. They keep us from reigning. As long as we keep believing we are not who God says we are, we won't step into our identity, and Satan knows it. We need to believe what God says about us.

So, what is our identity, and what does God have to say about who we are?

My friend has a great answer when he is asked, "How are you?" He replies, *"I am blessed,*[20] *highly favored,*[21] *and deeply loved."*[22] [23] This is how God sees us. This is what Scripture says about us—about you.

Remembering who He says we are based on Scripture gives us victory over the lies of the enemy, who is looking to continue his reign. Tonight, I spoke to my daughter about fear. There was a pretty loud thunderstorm at the time. It scared her. It didn't make matters any better that the radio station she was listening to noted the risk of tornadoes (in Massachusetts, mind you)!

I noticed her concern and asked her who it is that tries to make us afraid. Satan was her answer. Then I asked her, "What do we do when we are tempted to be afraid?" She got part of it. She noted that we rebuke fear and tell it to leave. She did that. The next part she was unsure of. This is the part where we are to declare the word of God, the truth, casting light on the lie, and standing on what God said. Her trouble was not the concept; it was her limited memorization of Scripture. She didn't know what verses to declare or stand on to war against the fear. She did not know what she was (or is) allowed to do. Once I shared some appropriate verses with

[20] Jeremiah 17:7

[21] Psalm 5:12

[22] John 3:16

[23] Dematos, Lee. Pastor of Indian Lake Church. From a personal conversation, 2019. Worcester, MA

her, she jumped on them and was able to use them to stand on, and her fear was gone.

I wish I had this when I was young. Even now, sometimes I falter.

I still work at reminding myself what God said and what the Bible says is true when the lies of Satan come to mind. I must recognize false thoughts and, in a way, "reprogram" my mind to be in agreement with His word, the truth which sets me free as I cast *"down imaginations, and every high thing that exalted itself against the knowledge of God, and bringing into captivity every thought to the obedience of Christ;"* (New King James, 2 Corinthians 10:5a)

Indeed, we all need to cast down every imagination and make our thoughts His thoughts, taking our worldly and doubting thoughts as captive servants, obedient to Christ.[24] We must have the mind of Christ.[25] If we do not, we can spiral into doubt and land in defeat.

Believing in lies holds us back.

The sins of our past that get in the way of us having the mind of Christ are covered in the blood of the Lamb. They are no more. They have been cast into the sea of forgetfulness[26] and are removed *"as far as the East is from the west."* (New International Version, Psalm 103:12) Holding onto them as a present reality hinders us from the spiritual freedom Jesus paid for on the cross. It also blocks us from stepping into the resurrection life that Jesus paid for us to have with Him.

---

[24] 2 Corinthians 10:5

[25] 1 Corinthians 2:16

[26] Micah 7:19

Our battle—our biggest battle—is overcoming the lies of the enemy about ourselves. We can only do this with the sword of the Spirit: The Word of God[27] which proclaims His victory and ours. With the sword, we can maintain daily and even minute-to-minute victory through a godly concept of ourselves.

We maintain our identity by remembering and proclaiming what the Word says about us.

You must study the Scriptures to learn what the Word says about you so that your thoughts align with His. As we ask the Holy Spirit to show us what God thinks of us He will show us. He loves us. He loves you.

He wants a restored relationship with you. He forgives you, as you are covered with the blood of Jesus. You are restored in Him.

You are His beloved child.[28]

Worthy in His eyes. [29]

---

[27] Ephesians 6:17
[28] 1 John 3

[29] John 3:16

Study Questions

1. If someone were to ask, "Who are you?" what would you say? Would you choose to share certain parts of your story?

2. Read 2 Corinthians 5:17. What might Satan have kept you believing about yourself that hindered you, accepting your identity in Christ?

3. Read 2 Corinthians 5:17, Jeremiah 17:7, and Psalm 5:12. What is our identity, and what does God have to say about who we are?

4. Forgiveness is available for all things in our pasts. What things might you bring before the Lord, asking Him to forgive?

7
In His Name

Making things right is the job of a King. A good king will win his battles with limited casualties and minimal recourse. Our King has done this.

He fought and won.

He won our freedom back, but importantly, He also won our authority back.

As I noted, authority is a key in this Kingdom as it is with all kingdoms. Actually, anyone doing business in the world, or in the Kingdom, must have and assert authority in order for others to listen to them.

Demons don't heed doubters.

I am not a police officer, so I cannot go downtown and command someone to go to jail. I also cannot command an army in battle. I am not a commander in the army. I am, however, a child of the King. This makes all the difference in the world—and in the Kingdom.

I have authority because I am His child.

When He rescued me, He also put me back into right standing in the Kingdom. He restored my authority as a child of God.

The King wants to raise all His children to understand that they have the same authority He does. The SAME authority as Jesus.

Now, before you get all riled up, I am not saying we are gods. BUT, I am saying we are sons and daughters of God, just like Jesus. In the Gospel of John, the writer says of Jesus: *"But as many as received Him, to them He gave the right to become children of God, to those who believe in His name."* (New King James, John 10:35) We who believe are those who are God's children.

Again, later in the New Testament, the parent/child concept is affirmed with these words: *"And 'I will be a Father to you, and you will be my sons and daughters, says the Lord Almighty.'"* (New International Version, 2 Corinthians 6:18)

Like Jesus, we can come under the Father and act in Jesus' stead in the earth, as His children. After all, He told the first humans to subdue and have dominion over the earth.[30] Doesn't this mean to reign over it?

Wait. Important side note: from whom did Adam and Eve take dominion? Satan.

Satan desired to be the ruler over this earth even before God's first children traded their authority to him for the fruit of the garden.

Satan was always where the people were, but that was *never* God's plan, nor was it His plan for Satan to rule. Satan was a servant, a messenger.

God always intended for His children to reign.

He always expected them to take His lead and use their authority over the earth as His children. Satan was supposed to be in heaven, serving God. Like us, he had the power of choice. His choice, like all choices, had consequences. Even with choices, Satan was never meant to and has no authority

---

[30] Genesis 1:28

to reign. God meant and means for us to do so.

He sent the Holy Spirit to help us overthrow the enemy, foil his plans, and take the land!

God wants to help us in our process of stepping into power and authority. Think about an earthly King, maybe Pharaoh. He would certainly raise up his own children to lead and then take over for him. As in Egypt, when the son or daughter of a king tells you to move, you move no matter how young the child is! You do this because of the child's relationship to the king. He is royal. It is the same in the Kingdom of Heaven. When the King's child tells even a mountain to move, it moves. It asks no questions; it just moves.[31]

The King wants His children to trust His victory and authority so much that they too can execute His will.

The King trains His children not to doubt either His authority or ours. We are His heirs. We come in His name.

Jesus taught us the same protocol. Jesus many times taught His disciples and followers to act in His name. He taught them to ask for things from the Father in His name[32], but also to cast out demons and lay hands on the sick so they would recover in His name.[33] He even taught His disciples that, as His children, they could raise the dead in His name.[34] His name is not a catchphrase to be added after an order or directive. In fact, as I noted earlier, saying His name isn't even

---

[31] Mt. 17:20

[32] John 14:12-14

[33] Mark 16:17-18

[34] Matthew 10:8

needed. It is an understood and indisputable truth in the Kingdom. We are to act in His stead.

Jesus trained His disciples through His actions and His words and gave them power to walk in this authority, as noted in Matthew, which reads, *"And when He had called His twelve disciples to Him, He gave them power over unclean spirits, to cast them out, and to heal all kinds of sickness and all kinds of disease."* (New King James, Mt. 10:1) Remember: The King is "away" in heaven, and we are His representatives on earth.

We are to act *like* Him and act *for* Him in His grace, power, and love.

We need to learn to act with the Holy Spirit on Jesus' behalf.

Like princes and princesses, we speak, heal, and command as He taught and as if He were here. Of this truth, Jesus said, *"Most assuredly, I say to you, the Son can do nothing of Himself, but what He sees the Father do; for whatever He does, the Son also does in like manner. For the Father loves the Son and shows Him all things that He Himself does; and He will show Him greater works than these, that you may marvel. For as the Father raises the dead and gives life to them, even so the Son gives life to whom He will."* (New King James, John 5:19-21)

We can do nothing without the authority given to us and the power of the Holy Spirit.

This is how the Kingdom works. The King teaches His children how to rule and then sends them to do so in His absence, just like cowboys.

Cowboys…? What? No, not the American football team—real cowboys!

Humor me for a moment. Cowboys, most often, have

been trained by their fathers and have been taught how to take care of cattle and the other animals, as well as how to manage the family business. A typical cowboy (or farmer) will teach his son the nuances of farming, raising, and herding, how to care for the animals and even how to do business for the ranch or farm. In fact, at some point, a father would tell a boy, "Okay, today you take the cows down to the river and then lead them back to the barn."

He will determine when he has sufficiently trained up his son in obedience and character and can trust him for the job. Then he will send him to do what he was taught. Later, the father will ask the son to go to town and do the father's business, to buy and sell in his name. He will also likely teach the boy to hunt and kill prey, then giving him a gun to protect the land, animals, and people.

Like a cowboy, God wants to raise up children to rule, protect, and take care of the Kingdom in His name obediently with God-like character.

We don't actually need to walk around saying, "In Jesus' name," whenever we are doing the King's business. If we are princes and princesses of the Kingdom, we just need to walk in the authority we already have and get the job done.

There is much work to be done or undone here on earth. This is why the King wants to train us up and send us out. Didn't He do just that? Jesus said, *"But go rather to the lost sheep of the house of Israel. "And as you go, preach, saying, 'The kingdom of heaven is at hand.' Heal the sick, cleanse the lepers, raise the dead, cast out demons. Freely you have received, freely give."* (New King James, Matthew 10:6-8)

As His children, not only do we have authority to move mountains and heal the sick, but we also have authority to do what Jesus said and whatever the Holy Spirit leads us to do.

Yes, *we* can and should drive out demons and raise the dead! I didn't make this up! He did. Jesus says in John 14:12 that *we will do even greater things* than the disciples saw Him do with the Holy Spirit. Christ's teaching isn't too lofty a goal to attain. Otherwise, why would He have said it? Did He not believe it was possible?

Didn't he believe in us if He told us to do it?

Didn't He expect us to follow through in faith, believing that what He said is true?

Jesus bought us and made us part of the Kingdom. Now He is training and sending. *We* must act.

This might be a complete paradigm shift, but it is at the core of the Kingdom's good news! We don't have to wait on God to do it. We can act out His will, take care of His creation, and love others in His stead.

I am not saying God cannot or does not act. Of course, there is providence. He does intervene at times. Still, He really wants us to walk out what He provided for and what He designed. He gave us the authority and mission because He wants the work done. He wants His children healed, free, and reinstalled as rulers under Him, just as we were intended to be in the beginning.

God wants a partnership.

He wants to participate and watch like a proud papa as we follow through on His instructions and glorify Him in doing so.

It is hard in the flesh and in this world to believe there is a Kingdom; I get it. There aren't a lot of believers walking in such authority, nor are there many pastors preaching on it, but we long for it. Again, this is why we have so many fairy tales with happy endings. We have a King, and we have a real enemy, but to consider overthrowing false rulers—that is a hard thing! It takes faith in the unseen and in God's words. Maybe that is why even in the Scriptures, people struggled so much to believe.

In this world, it can seem easier for some to accept the reality of other principalities, gods, or even Satan than God the Father. Sometimes it seems easier to not consider any of this, or even to deny it all. For those who do believe in the one true God, it seems more common to accept the concept that His ways are too difficult to understand and it is too much work to seek them out. But God desires for us to keep seeking them out. His ways are higher than our ways, and His thoughts, higher than ours. [35]

We must press on and press in to understand the good news, including all its power and authority for us from Him.

Our authority is part of the Good News!

We must learn what it means to stand in authority, believe God's promises, and fulfill the needs of the Kingdom. It is time to wear our crowns of salvation[36] in the battle instead of the typical battle helmets because *we are to fight in the spiritual, not the physical.* As we do, we will stand on God's Word and His promises of capability and authority. For example, God teaches we can lay hands on the sick and they will be healed. We have to trust Him and walk that out, perhaps initially failing as we learn, just like any child.

One of the ways we walk in the authority of the

---

[35] Is. 55: 9

[36] Eph 6:17

Kingdom is to carry out His will by healing the sick. Healing the sick sometimes seems daunting or complicated. So many are sick! Even priests and pastors suffer. Healing ministers suffer. Infirmity is real. Sickness is real. But the command to heal is also real. It is because of sickness, disease, and infirmity that there is a need for healing.

God loves His children and those who are His. It is not His desire for anyone to be sick.

I know there are so many dialogues that could go on right here. There is the conversation about those that never were healed, those that aren't healed yet, and those that weren't able to heal others when they tried. There is the dialogue about God using all things and Him making all things work out *"for the good of those who love Him."* (New International Version, Romans 8:28) I get it. When things don't work the way we think, it is hard, but it is never God's preference for His beloved to get or stay sick.

Never.

God wouldn't have healed, taught on healing, or commissioned us to heal the sick if He wanted the sickness to remain. In His Word we can read many stories showing He did heal people.

He taught His disciples to heal others.

Faith in healing is made more difficult by the lack of healing testimonies in circulation. There are testimonies, but they are not heard every day since the media has negated them, criticized them, and even made healing seem fabricated. Many stories of healing go without much press. Yet if you search, you can find real stories of healing.

This is what brought people to the Kingdom in the first place. When gawkers and onlookers saw the healings, they followed Jesus and then the disciples.

I have seen and experienced real healings. I desire many more, but as I have learned to walk with the Lord and learn, I find that when I look, I see more. I have also had my own body instantly healed at the hand of a Baptist pastor and his wife. I went from not being able to lift my legs to get into my car so I could go to Easter service, to dancing in my uncle's kitchen—within about a half hour of their prayers.

I have also seen others healed as I did what I have been taught—to heal the sick in Jesus' name. I prayed for a girl who had asthma, commanding the sickness to go and healing to come. Her mother told me she has not had asthma since.

I prayed for a man whose hands had pain (and who needed to continue to play guitar for a conference), commanding the pain and tingling to leave, declaring healing would come and that he would play for the Lord. His hands were instantly healed. He played for the rest of the evening as planned.

Another woman had allergies to foods, which became less problematic after prayer.

I have also walked out healing myself, declaring I was not going to get a headache when my "typical" migraine symptoms began. When dizziness came, I stood on the Lord's promises of authority, believing there is power I could exercise in the spiritual Kingdom of Heaven. I believed I did not have to accept a headache. I declared I would not need medicine or a sitter for my children (which would have been necessary in the past based on the symptoms). I decided not even to call my mother to come help, nor did I take any medicine. I just went on with life as if I were healed. It was a decision to stand on and walk out my faith and truth of the

Kingdom in its reality.

The Lord paid for my healing.

Jesus paid for all healing.

I have authority to cast out sickness and disease. I chose to believe this and declare it—to refuse that headache. It did not come.

I am not always perfect or successful in this, but I press on in faith.

We can proclaim His word and promises over the situation, and the situation will change.

The healing will come.

The mountain will move.

We must stand in faith that what our Father said is true, no matter what.

Even if the symptoms or the doctor's tests might indicate otherwise, we must believe the Lord. Those symptoms are not part of the Kingdom. They are from the enemy. I know they feel very real and powerful, but they and those who bring them have been rendered powerless.

Are we perfect at this yet? No. Few, if any, have a 100% healing record. Still, so many have story after story of healings and deliverance. Even the disciples struggled as they learned to do what Jesus taught them to.

The Bible records that the father of an epileptic boy brought his son to the disciples to be healed. He later told Jesus, *"So I brought him to Your disciples, but they could not cure him."* Then Jesus answered and said, *'O faithless and perverse generation, how long shall I be with you? How long shall I bear with you? Bring him here to Me.'* And Jesus rebuked the demon, and it *came out of him; and the child was cured from that very hour. Then the disciples came to Jesus privately and said, 'Why could we not cast it out?' So Jesus said to them, 'Because of your unbelief; for assuredly, I say to you, if you have faith as a mustard seed, you will say to this mountain, 'Move from here to there,' and it will move; and nothing will be impossible for you. However, this kind does not go out except by prayer and fasting.'"* (New International Version, Matthew 17:16-21)

The disciples didn't understand at first. They thought they were doing what the Lord had shown them, but they were missing faith—missing a belief in the authority God gave them. They weren't fully walking in the authority available to them. Instead, they were heeding the lie of Satan, who taunts people, hoping it will create unbelief. The biggest enemy of our faith is the same liar he was in the beginning. Satan's lies still work.

"Did God really say…?" (New International Version, Genesis 3:1)

Don't we all hear that same taunting? We wonder if God really wants to heal or deliver. Is it all real? Did He give *us* enough authority to get the job done? Who are we anyway?

Did God really say? Did He really say *that*?

Part of learning is to push past the taunting (or to tell Satan to go) and carry on with the task we were given, believing our Father more than the enemy. Our Father wants us to believe we can do all things because we stand in faith regarding who He is and who He says we are.

We *can* do what He sent us to do.

It isn't that God doesn't believe in *us*, but that we don't believe in ourselves. He believes we can heal in His name and with the Spirit's power. Otherwise, why would He have told us to do any of this?

He already believes in me! In you! This is part of the good news—all of this!

This is Kingdom reality!

Study Questions

1. We have the same authority as Jesus, but what authority does He have? See Matthew 28:18 and Mark 1:27.

2. Read Genesis 1:28. With the same authority, how might we reign over the earth with Him?

3. When things don't work the way we think, it is hard. How have you walked in faith and felt it didn't bring the results you hoped for?

4. Read Genesis 3:1. How has doubt entered our mind, or beliefs when things didn't go as you believed?

8
Warfare

A good king wants to raise His children to rule well.

As the good king, God wants us to grow and learn to be more and more like Him, serving others in the Kingdom with the selfless love of Jesus and then showing others what He is like by example. He wants us to love sacrificially and serve—to care for weary and broken people like Jesus did. But that's not all. It isn't *only* about love.

Kings train up their children to reign… and reigning requires power because there is war! Every story about a kingdom has a battle! This one does too. We see it.

What is the Good Father teaching us, His children, about warfare?

We must learn about this fight.

We must learn how to defend ourselves during battle and then how to overtake and maintain victory - to advance. This is what the armor of God is for.[37]

Some might jump to the complete victory of the Lord and stand on that, believing there is no fight remaining, but I assure you, the fight is still on. We are in it daily, and our enemy *"prowls around like a roaring lion, seeking whom he may devour."* (New King James, 1 Peter 5:8) He is Lucifer, the fallen one, and he is still fighting. We need to suit up and get ready.

---
[37] Ephesians 6:10-18

The battle is at hand all around us, even if we cannot yet see the Kingdom or the victory. Sickness, disease, trauma, brokenheartedness, selfishness, murder, and strife—we all see and experience it. In our spirits, we know these things are not good.

We know there should be victory.

We are called, at times, to focus on who the enemy is and understand that *we* are actually the ones carrying out and *fulfilling* the victory.

We are to learn our Father's goals, how to enact the fulfillment of those goals, and how to advance and facilitate His plans to set captives free (sometimes we must even set ourselves free before or even in the midst of battle, walking in the freedom He paid for.) We are to learn how to fight for ourselves and others. How do we begin? We must study His ways and His Word.

Strangely, fighting in the Kingdom and in the Word doesn't really look like fighting in this world. God's method of fighting isn't what we would think of as fighting. It's not hand-to-hand combat. There are no guns. Surprisingly, we are to stand in God's truth with peace, His word, and His victory.

In doing that, we actually gain our victory as well.

We have an enemy.

There is a live and active supernatural population, part of which, having fallen, is at war with us. Though it may appear as if we fight against flesh and blood, we do not. No. Our fight is not against the people we rub shoulders with, *"but against the rulers, against the authorities, against the powers of this dark world and against the spiritual forces of evil in the heavenly realms."* (New International Version, Ephesians 6:12)

Right now, these forces bring division. They work to change and negatively impact thinking, manipulate circumstances, and attack physically. They expert control over the geographical area, and shape spheres of influence.

For this reason, we need to learn how to fight, to fight God's way, and learn attentively from Him.

If we do not stay aware of the enemy's advances, we risk being overtaken. Picture the Karate Kid blocking every advance... *"Wax on, wax off.*[38]*"* With each lie, we react with truth. Furthermore, with each attack, we must react with authority.

Authority! It is so crucial that we understand this.

We MUST walk in authority and advance against the enemy.

Why is authority so important? Remember, we are talking about the Kingdom. Within this Kingdom, there are levels or ranks, just as there is with any earthly kingdom. In the Kingdom of God, God is the head, then the angels, then us as *"a little lower than the angels"*—at least for now. (New International Version, Psalm 8:5)

Well, not *all* the angels.

We are not *supposed* to be under (obedient to) the fallen angels. Likewise, we are not to be under the demons. We were *never* meant to follow them as *"sheep led to slaughter."*[39]

Are fallen angels demons? No, but the specifics could take up many books. Let me simply note that demons are supernatural creatures on the earth, and in the second heaven.[40]

---

[38] Avildsen, Bill Conti & Brooks Arthur. (1984) The Karate Kid. USA.

[39] Isaiah 53:7 and Romans 8:36

They are some of the forces attempting to come against us and wanting to help Satan dethrone God's children.

Demons are subject to us[41] and to the sword of the Spirit. As we learn and come into agreement with our authority within the Kingdom, wielding our sword, which is the Word of God, we can use that authority to reign over these demonic forces, renouncing their impact on us.

As noted in Ephesians 6, we are given and are told to take up a sword for this battle; it is the sword of the Spirit, the word of God, *"sharper than a double-edged sword."* (New International Version, Hebrews 4:12)

The sword is the only offensive weapon in the armor of God,[42] but this weapon is not used in the traditional way we think.

In Hebrews, the writer is not referring to a long sword we might generally associate with fighting. The word in the Greek is *machaira (μάχαιρα)*. These were smaller, curved knives used for sacrifice, judgment, and close defense. The *machaira* is a surprisingly fierce and powerful defensive weapon with a bend in the tip. In combat, the user uses two hands to thrust and then twist, thereby emptying the enemy and giving him no hope of retaliation.

The sword of the Spirit is like the *machaira* because it, too, is the perfect weapon. It is no wonder Scripture uses this type of sword to communicate that there is no hope for the enemy when *this* sword is handled well.

---

[40] Revelation 21:1, 2 Corinthians 12:2

[41] Mark 3:15

[42] Ephesians 6:17

Strong's Concordance says the *machaira* was *"an instrument for exacting retribution."*[43] This may be true since it was a precise weapon to be feared, but surprisingly, it was also known to be a type of self-care tool used in battle to dig out other weapons like arrow heads from the body. So, the *machaira* would remove whatever was thrown at the warrior.

We need to use the Word of God to refute the lies of Satan and the weapons of his warfare. We must remove the lies the enemy uses in battle regarding the truth of who God is and who He says we are. Just as he questioned Jesus in the wilderness about His identity and authority, we must have answers for ours which we can only garner from His Word.[44]

Using God's Word in battle is most powerful when it flows from our own mouths. These swords of retribution are to swish and move with power like tongues of fire. The Lord is seen with a sword in His mouth in Revelation.[45] We are to speak the Word as well. We are to keep His Word, the sword, ready in our mouths, in our minds, but also in our hearts.

Culturally, the *machaira* swords are said to have been *"kept in special places and used in important rituals"* ("Machaira")[46] and saved for kings or priests. In the Kingdom, we who are priests and kings, are to hold the Word of God sacred as we advance.

Jesus chose specific words to communicate effectively

---

[43] Strong, James. Strong's Exhaustive Concordance of the Bible. Abingdon Press, 1890. Strong's Concordance. https://biblehub.com/greek/3162.htm

[44] Matthew 4

[45] Revelation 19:15

[46] "Machaira". Wikipedia. Wikipedia Foundation. June, 2020. https://simple.wikipedia.org/wiki/Machaira

regarding these things. Because of this, I want to take just a moment to focus on Jewish culture in order to increase understanding, specifically regarding *this* particular and crucial sword of the Spirit and its many uses in battle.

We cannot neglect our *machaira*.

In biblical history, the culture surrounding the words of the Bible isn't the same today. So many things are different. Therefore, learning about context is critical for accurate and true biblical translation and understanding.

Let me draw your attention to the ancient Hebrew letters. Hebrew letters were not just letters. They were represented numbers and were images that told a story. The letter *Zayin*, for example, also represented the number seven.

Zayin[47]

Interestingly, this seven looked like a sword, and what's more, a sword with a crown. This *zayin*, the sword with a crown, would have been in the mind of every educated Jew, perhaps even Greeks. Both the scholar and fisherman, if they could read and write, would likely know the Hebrew letters and the pictorial story they represented. It was part of their culture and communication.

Why is this significant?

Don't check out... There is a point to this sword.

---

[47] Parsons, John J. *The Letter Zayin*, The Letter Zayin, hebrew4christians.com/Grammar/Unit_One/Aleph-Bet/Zayin/zayin.html.

The Hebrew4christians.com website notes, *'"Zayin is a paradoxical word, since it means "weapon" or "sword", but derives from a root word that means "sustenance" or "nourishment"'*[48]

Stay with me! There is even more to this sword!

Sustenance! Nourishment!

This *machaira*, the Word of God, also represents food!

We all know food is important. Fasting can be hard and even a bit ugly. When Jesus fasted, what did he say about food? He said to them, "I have food to eat that you know nothing about." (New International Version, John 4:32) We might think he snuck in some manna or that the angels fed Him, but no!

The Passion translation of the Bible clarifies in its footnotes for John 4:32 in speaking about having food to eat as it reads, *'"There is a fascinating word play here in the Aramaic. The word Jesus uses isn't the common word for "food", but is actually a word that means nutrients." It is also a homonym that is more commonly translated "kingdom." Jesus has a kingdom feast that no one else knows about."'*[49]

What was Christ's nourishment during battle against the enemy? The Word of God, which is the sword of the Spirit, perhaps even a crowned sword. This is the children's bread!! He is! The Word of God is our bread!

In the desert, the tempter came to Jesus and said, *"If you are the Son of God, tell these stones to become bread."* Jesus answered, *"It is written: 'Man does not live on bread alone, but on*

---

[48] Parsons, John J. *The Letter Zayin,* The Letter Zayin, hebrew4christians.com/Grammar/Unit_One/Aleph-Bet/Zayin/zayin.html.

[49] The Passion Translation, Copyright 2017, 2018; Passion & Fire Ministries, Inc., Page 593, Notation

every word that comes from the mouth of God.'" (New International Version, Matthew 4:3-4)

He ate the word of God—the truth.

In battle, the sword is our defense, our self-care, and our sustenance! We survive and thrive by partaking of and using God's Word for our nourishment and protection. His Word demolishes every argument *"and every pretension that sets itself up against the knowledge of God, and we take captive every thought to make it obedient to Christ."* (New International Version, 2 Corinthians 10:5)

His Word assists us as we fight and sustains us through our battles. The Word of God demolishes every stronghold. These strongholds are agreements put in place because mankind has trusted the enemy for protection instead of God and His authority.

When we learn and believe His Word, denoting our authority and God's love, strongholds are defeated and no longer hold power.

The sword of the Spirit is the Word of God. It is living and active. It is also the nourishing and sustaining bread of life, the Messiah, of whom we are to *"take and eat."* (New International Version, Matthew 26:26)

We need to remember and partake of Him, and even in the midst of battle, we are to remind ourselves and the enemy of Christ's finished work. We take in perfect sustenance in front of Satan. The Lord is the table set before us in front of our enemy.[50]

With this *machaira*, His Word, Jesus Himself, we have such victory that we can sit at the table during the battle as

---

[50] Psalm 23:5

God meets all our needs.

What an overt act of retaliation!

Even as we take communion, we lift *THE* sword and proclaim His victory and our victory in Him. Like Jesus, we proclaim and stand in our authority. With each attack, we respond with the word that contradicts every lie.

This is the fight to preserve our thought life. We fight to retain the mind of Christ. We align our mind with His Word. We maintain and present the remembrance of Christ's victory and our authority with every wave of the sword and every bite of bread.

Scripture notes: *"The weapons we fight with are not the weapons of the world. On the contrary, they have divine power to demolish strongholds. We demolish arguments and every pretension that sets itself up against the knowledge of God, and we take captive every thought to make it obedient to Christ."* (New International Version, 2 Corinthians 10:4-5)

We demolish arguments with God's truth and our authority as we sit at His table as His children.

The spiritual beings we fight understand the truth of the Word and respond to authority. They know they need to obey Jesus. They obeyed the disciples, too, once the disciples understood their authority—the authority Jesus gave them.[51]

When the disciples began trusting God's Word in battle, the forces of evil began to obey. This happened before Pentecost, so we aren't talking about Spirit-filled Christians. No, these are the ones who had authority even before Jesus died! They are the ones who used their authority to drive out demons and heal the sick. They aligned themselves with the

---
[51] Matthew 10:1

truth, which then brought alignment in Kingdom authority.

In Jesus, we have the same authority as His disciples. We have and are supposed to take up this authority to reign in the Kingdom. In His Word, Jesus specifically told us to even rebuke Satan and drive out demons as He did.[52]

Demons need to go!

These enemies aren't supposed to be running amok in victory. Believers are supposed to be resisting them,[53] binding them,[54] and sending them out from our presence. When we become aware of their presence, their attacks, or their manipulation, we can and must rebuke them *with our swords!*

We declare the truth of God's Word, and tell them to go... Some people add, "in Jesus' name!" I used to do this, but then I realized it is understood, so I don't always do this. The demons know I am His, and they know my rights. I need not explain. They must obey me because of who I am in the Kingdom. They know I have authority, and I must wield it.

Think of it: does the prince of England walk around explaining he is the prince? Does he have to carry an ID and declare he acts under his parents' authority? No. It is already understood by the people.

As God's child, I need not explain my authority.

You don't need to either.

This authority is the victory played out and used to drive out demons, heal the sick and raise the dead. It can also command the wind and the waves and even move mountains

---

[52] Matthew 10:8

[53] James 4:7

[54] Matthew 12:29

in His name.

This is why Jesus said, *"Truly I tell you, if you have faith as small as a mustard seed, you can say to this mountain, 'Move from here to there,' and it will move. Nothing will be impossible for you."* (New International Version, Matthew 17:20)

Nothing.

Study Questions

1. Every story about a kingdom has a battle. How has the battle gone for you? In what ways has it wearied you?

2. Read Matthew 16:19, Mark 1:27 and Revelation 2:26. What does it mean to walk in authority and advance against the enemy?

3. We are to keep His Word, the sword, ready in our mouths, in our minds, but also in our hearts. Psalms 119:11 notes, "I have stored up your word in my heart, that I might not sin against you." How have you been storing up His Word in your mind and heart?

4. We have victory when we sit at the table during the battle, as God meets all our needs. How might God be leading you to rest and let His victory bring yours based on Proverbs 3:5-6, Matthew 28:11, and Hebrews 4:1-11?

9
Children Listen

Our heavenly Father communicates with us. He wants to. He actually desires to have a relationship with us all. It is why He created us.

Children in a healthy family know their father's voice because their father talks to them. Once we are covered with the blood of the sinless Lamb, we can have that relationship with our Father, for our sin is no longer in need of judgment.

We are the Father's children by choice.

The Father chooses to have a relationship with us and wants us to know His voice so He can love on us, lead us, and teach us. Our Father, the King, is always communicating. Thankfully, communication can be learned, but learning God's ways of communication takes time, just as it takes time to learn His Word.

The teachable disciples asked Jesus how to communicate in prayer. Jesus replied with what we now call the Lord's Prayer, saying, *"When you pray, say: Our Father in heaven, hallowed be your name. Your kingdom come. Your will be done on earth as it is in heaven. Give us day by day our daily bread."* (New King James, Luke 11:2-3) Jesus willingly taught them, putting things in the context of family and unity. He didn't reply in anger, telling them that by now they should have known how to pray. Though Christ did get saddened or frustrated at times, He still patiently taught them.

Even if Jesus has to teach us again and again, He will.

He does.

How are we taught? We are taught through Scripture, prayer, life lessons, and listening to others in the Kingdom. We can read what the Word has to say about the Kingdom and then test it out. As we do, we learn we can rely on the Word for life and direction. Life lessons also provide teaching.

Sometimes these lessons are the hardest because we stumble as we learn.

Mistakes happen, but still we learn.

I don't want to leave out one of the most important ways of learning from and communicating with the LORD. As believers, we were given a Teacher who dwells within each of us as believers. The Holy Spirit, or "the Comforter" (the Spirit of God), was sent from the Lord specifically to guide and assist us.

The Holy Spirit is the best life coach ever.

He provides 100% accuracy with compassion and is available 24 hours a day, 365 days a year. Furthermore, the Holy Spirit is gracious and kind, convicting us of the need for change, but without condemnation.

As we pray (which just means to talk and be attentive to God's response), we can listen for and heed the Holy Spirit's promptings. He will teach us how to carry out our role in the Kingdom and how to care for the things of God. We need Him!

Maybe you have heard the Holy Spirit speak, or maybe you're thinking, "I have no idea how to talk with, let alone hear, the Holy Spirit." Actually, He is always interacting, always wanting you to notice and heed His suggestions. Part of what the Lord wants to teach you is how to pick up on His communication because the Holy Spirit doesn't speak the way we do, at least not generally. He doesn't usually communicate with an audible, external voice. This is one reason why so many say they have never heard Him.

Like any parent, the Holy Spirit does at times speak audibly (externally) like man. Most often, though, He speaks in other ways that sound internal. His voice can be so familiar that it sounds like your own. Many people say they thought they were just hearing themselves at first.

One key to discerning His voice is that the Holy Spirit's good advice often seems surprising or even contrary to an initial human reaction in a situation.

The Holy Spirit can be subtle with His promptings and gentle guidance. His communication is similar to the facial communication of a parent to a child. Small facial movements can be a big deal in such communication because of the close familial relationship. In the same way, the Spirit's promptings can be feelings, downloaded imagination, or thoughts, even imagery (visions).

Sometimes communicating with the Holy Spirit is like following a road map, a treasure map, or a trail of breadcrumbs.

Can this be frustrating? Sure.

Usually, we want a yes or no, left, or right, as with a global positioning system. However, following the Holy Spirit can be an amazing treasure hunt because, within the Kingdom, *"It is the glory of God to conceal a matter; to search out a matter is the glory of kings..."* (New International Version, Proverbs 25:2) Every bit of communication with God is well worth it, but it requires us to remain actively connected with Him in order for us to hear or understand His messages.

It takes time to get to know someone.

Knowing the Holy Spirit requires a decision to tune into and learn His voice, His ways, and His methods. In some ways, it is like learning the ways of a new spouse; it's a journey of entering into a relationship.

What are some ways people hear the Holy Spirit?

There are many. For starters, He speaks through a still small voice, visions, dreams, promptings, and feelings.

Humans use more than just words to communicate. Our communication is intricate. Not only do we communicate with words, but also with facial expressions, body language, and many other indirect nuances. Should the Lord not have even more vast and creative methods of communication?

The Holy Spirit communicates in many different ways.

We need to be attentive to Him and learn the sound of the Holy Spirit (our Shepherd's) voice and His methods of communication, even if it is through the song on the radio or words of a prophet. Sometimes His methods are surprising. They surprise me.

At one time, my husband and I were considering purchasing a house. The house was a fixer-upper and a foreclosure. Though we had plans to change much of it and renovate, there were many times I felt overwhelmed with the process and doubtful of our decision. During one of these moments, I felt so weary that I just wanted out. I wanted to forget it all and stay in our starter home.

One night during the process, I was scurrying around as a short-order cook for my three children at dinner time. I was frustrated and distracted. It was not a time when I was giving the Lord my attention. I was grumbling to Him but not expecting a response.

In the midst of all of this, I was suddenly captivated by a song on the radio. Before that I had not been paying attention to the music because I was busy, but in the next moment, I was 100% focused on the song, and it was as if the world stopped.

Elton John's voice came through all my static, and I heard the lyrics, *"I'd buy a big house where we both could live..."* I broke! Tears everywhere!

Moments later, I heard... *"And you can tell everybody this is your song. It may be quite simple, but now that it's done, I hope you don't mind, I hope you don't mind that I put down in words how wonderful life is while you're in the world."*[55]

I was undone. I knew it was Him. It was perfectly timed, and I could feel His love surrounding me.

We bought the house.

How did I know it was a message from Him? That is a valid question. The Bible teaches us to *"test everything. Hold on to the good."* (New International Version, 1 Thessalonians 5:21) and in 1 John He says, *"Beloved, do not believe every spirit, but test the spirits, whether they are of God; because many false prophets have gone out into the world."* (New King James, 1 John 4:1) In this testing everything against the truth of His word, we make sure what we think we hear, feel, or see lines up with examples in the past depicted in God's Word and His character as shared through the Word of God.

---

[55] Elton John. "Your Song." May 20, 2020.
https://www.azlyrics.com/lyrics/eltonjohn/yoursong.html

The King wants to communicate with His children.

Any good father would, right? We need to believe it and take time to listen for the Lord's communication with us, even if we aren't sure what to look for initially.

I have known the Lord to communicate in many different ways. For me He speaks through dreams, visions, promptings, and songs. He also nudges me to be aware of things in my everyday life—interactions with the world around me that the Lord wants to highlight.

If I pay attention, pray, or talk to Him and listen, the Lord will expound on what He is showing me. It might not be at that exact moment, but I will hear when I need to and am open to His voice.

I know everyone wants to hear ten easy steps to hearing from God. It isn't that cut and dried. It is a dance, a relational learning process.

Look for Him. Listen for Him.

Learn the ways He speaks with you.

God actually communicates with each of His children differently, just like an earthly father would, as He shares life and teaches each child with things that "speak" specifically to that child. My daughter, for example, learns best through songs. She and I sing-talk to each other sometimes, as we "love on" one another. She prays and worships with songs she writes. I am sure the Lord will continue to use that method to communicate with her. I also learn and memorize songs very quickly, so the Lord uses songs to communicate with me. However, I am primarily a visual person. Because of this, He most often shows me pictures in dreams and visions or highlights something I see in my surroundings, like a cardinal, to show me something. He does this kind of thing because it makes sense to me.

God's ways of communicating with you are likely to be very different. Maybe you are visual, or maybe you are auditory and will best hear Him audibly. God is always communicating in many ways. Why don't we notice Him? Doubt and distraction.

Not only do we often doubt we hear him, but distraction is also a huge hindrance to hearing God. It is like the conversation around the dinner table at my house. When I am not paying attention, I sometimes miss out on some of his communication. At times, it is hard for my husband and I to communicate with all the kids talking, laughing, and tapping their utensils. When we get away together in quietness, we can not only hear one another, but we can also pay attention to the nuances of our communication methods.

With the Holy Spirit, we are no different. We need to give Him attention without distraction as best we can throughout each day. As we are showering, sipping our coffee, driving, and even going to the bathroom, we can find moments where we are not distracted.

I almost wrote that God is waiting to communicate, but really, He is communicating even if you are not paying attention in hopes that you will notice and respond. Thankfully, God is patient. He just keeps on trying. His word reads that God even sings over us. [56]

Listen.

Can you hear Him?

---

[56] Zephaniah 3:17

Study Questions

1. As per Joel 2:28-29, John 14:26, and John 16:13, how does the Holy Spirit communicate?

2. How have you recognized the Holy Spirit communicating in your life?

3. Doubt can be one of the biggest hinderances to listening, as in Matthew 14:22-33,   and James 1:6. How does doubt hinder faith as you walk with the Lord?

4. The Lord noted things that get us off track in our walks per Matthew 6:31-33, and Colossians 3:1-2. What might be distracting you from the truth He is communicating?

10
Children Are Teachable

Jesus only did what He saw the Father doing.[57] Like Him, we have to be paying attention, teachable, and walk out what we have been taught.

To do anything at all, we must learn how. Even to walk or talk requires learning. Of course, I understand there is nature as well as nurture, but many things must be taught.

Wisdom is a good example of something that is taught in the Kingdom. In fact, God the King felt so strongly about wisdom that He devoted the whole book of Proverbs to it, never mind all the other teachings within the Bible about wisdom.

There are so many things the Lord wants to teach us. Countless things!

He wants to teach us about Himself and how He loves us. God also wants to teach us how to love, heal, prayerfully mend broken hearts, cast out demons, and then share all this good news!

God is a teacher!

He also wants to teach us how to create things and care for the earth. All these things are waiting to be taught.

We must be willing to be taught; being teachable is a decision.

---
[57] John 5:19

We all need to decide to be willing to be taught and to accept that we actually need teaching. This means being willing to consider that we don't already know everything. Even at salvation, we had to realize that what we first believed about God was a lie. Many people initially believe God doesn't care for them, then later learn He does. They are awakened to the need for God and the reality of human sinfulness.

At some point, God's children learn they need Him.

For those not raised as Christians, this can indeed be an awakening. Many have had to humbly repent (change their minds) in order to be ready and willing to come under Jesus as the necessary payment for sin.

Humility is something we humans really struggle with and always have. We must make the decision, moment by moment, to be humble. By being humble, we allow ourselves to come under someone else, to choose their ways instead of our own, or, in this case, to follow the Lord and be teachable.

We need to be willing to be led.

There is a song in my head now. The song is from James, which reads, *"Humble yourselves in the sight of the Lord, and He will lift you up."* (New International Version, James 4:10) Maybe you're humming along too. We need to humble ourselves so we can be tutored by our brother Jesus, the Holy Spirit and our King. It is a life-altering decision to humble ourselves under our brother Jesus and to learn from His example of the Father, our King.

It has always been hard for children to yield to authority, especially their big brother's authority. Scripture gives example after example of brothers who refused humility in relation to their brother. Think of Cain and Abel in Genesis 4.

God let Cain know that sin was crouching at his door. Cain had the opportunity to learn from his brother; maybe ask the Lord or Abel how to bring what was acceptable. Instead, He coveted a relationship in which he could freely have developed himself and chose sin in his anger. Like the angry older brother of the prodigal son parable in Luke 15, who already had everything but refused to come humbly to his Father, Cain was unwilling to be taught.

Even many of the Jews who did walk alongside Jesus refused to listen to their younger Brother. They believed they knew better, and that Jesus was not God and should do their bidding, heeding their "wisdom" instead of humbly heeding His. We must also follow and obey our Brother, letting Him lead. To do so, we must humble ourselves and become teachable.

There is no other way.

Jesus is the door—the only door. Humility is the key.

Only a humble person would cover himself with His brother's blood so that he could be forgiven and enter back into his Father's Kingdom. Only a humble brother (or sister) would listen to and heed a brother's leadership and wisdom.

Within the Kingdom, we choose to be humble, teachable, and come under the Lord in all three expressions of His nature. We decide to come under the love, rule, and reign of our Father. We willingly heed the example of our Brother and walk in the teaching and leading of the Holy Spirit.

If we want to thrive in and experience all the Kingdom of God has to offer, we need to be humble. Humility is part of Kingdom royalty. Traditionally, those who are knighted for their service bow down in honor and submission. Likewise, even children of a king bow to their father and mother.

We must bow down so He can raise us up.

Study Questions

───────────

1. How is being teachable a decision?

2. In the Lord's Prayer from Matthew 6 Jesus taught us how to pray saying "Our Father in heaven, hallowed be your name. Your kingdom come, your will be done, on earth as it is in heaven. Give us this day our daily bread, and forgive us our debts, as we also have forgiven our debtors. And lead us not into temptation, but deliver us from evil." In what ways do we need the Lord to lead us every day?

3. Humility is a huge factor in being teachable. How has humility been a struggle in your life?

4. If you feel the need, perhaps this is a time to repent of and ask for forgiveness for any pride that has gotten in your way of listening.

11
God Wants to Teach Us

God's Word reveals many things He wants us to learn. To write them all would be to rewrite the Bible. However, I wish to highlight some things that I feel are on His heart.

He is a Father. Like a good father, He wants to equip and raise up children to be proud of. He is pleased with His creations, both male and female, because He created them in His image and likeness, and they are good. He enjoys interacting with humans, and He sees our potential and value. In fact, He determines our value.

He considers us worthy of His care, attention, and love.

As a good Father, He wants to restore, equip, and refine us with the goal of populating and advancing His Kingdom. Our refining is a process of cleansing us of sin and darkness and re-establishing us in the image in which He created us: His.

He wants to bring us out of the darkness, rescuing us from the evil one, and clothing us with Salvation.[58] He wants to robe us in righteousness. He has always covered His children; He even clothed Adam and Eve before He sent them out of the garden.[59]

Our Father wants us to be clothed in the divine and

---
[58] Isaiah 61:10

[59] Genesis 3:21

supernatural beauty of His Holiness. He desires to *fill us with the Holy Spirit* and give us capabilities we can only obtain through His equipping. These capabilities are the gifts of the Spirit, which include wisdom and knowledge as well as miracles, healing, prophecy, tongues, and the fear of the Lord, as noted in 1 Corinthians 12. He wants to equip us with these gifts and teach us how to use them for others in the Kingdom. God, through the Holy Spirit, wants to guide us in doing so. Look here:

Scripture notes, *"There are different kinds of gifts, but the same Spirit distributes them."* Later it continues, *"Now to each one the manifestation of the Spirit is given for the common good. To one there is given through the Spirit a message of wisdom, to another a message of knowledge by means of the same Spirit, to another faith by the same Spirit, to another gifts of healing by that one Spirit, to another miraculous powers, to another prophecy, to another distinguishing between spirits, to another speaking in different kinds of tongues, and to still another the interpretation of tongues. All these are the work of one and the same Spirit, and he distributes them to each one, just as he determines."* (New International Version, 1 Corinthians 12:4; 7-11)

God wants us equipped.

The Lord wants us to have these gifts and know how to use them for the Body, the Church, and His Kingdom. He wants to bless His people with gifts so that the Church is healthy and thriving. We need to be willing to receive and use these gifts. This requires acceptance first and then training as we learn how to use them. These, like any gifts, are to be unpacked and put to use.

When the Church does not understand or use these gifts well, brokenness and pain remain in the Body. The gifts are useful to assist others to increase in health and freedom.

When I was a young Christian, I was often surprised that people liked to tell me their stories. This still happens. My husband often comments that people always share their stories with me, but they don't do that with him. Often, I also have surprisingly good advice. (I say surprisingly because it is from the Holy Spirit, and it often even surprises me.) At this point, I have realized this is a gift of prophecy and counsel. These are part of my calling and gifts.

Early on, even as a youth, I just thought it was me. As I grew, I realized it was the Holy Spirit. He was leading me to connect with people so He could help them. He was speaking through me. He wanted people to feel heard and gain help. The Holy Spirit wanted to speak through me to lead others to their next place. This is one of my gifts. It is not for me, but these kinds of gifts are for His kingdom and the body of Christ within it.

God equipped my husband with different gifts of worship, peace, and love. When people are with him, they feel comfortable, accepted, and loved. They are led to reflect on God's goodness. This gift is also for the Body. These are outward-turning gifts which assist and support others in the body, and it is more than the five-fold ministry.[60] We all have at least one if not many *"for the building up of the Body."* (English Standard Version, Ephesians 4:12)

For the health of the Body, God has provided what He calls fruit. This fruit is the outward sign of an internal and outworking sufficiency from the Holy Spirit. As we learn to hear and heed the Spirit, His gifts come forth for the provision of the Body. The fruits of the Spirit are *"love, joy, peace, patience, kindness, goodness, faithfulness, gentleness and self-control..."*

---

[60] Ephesians 4:11

(New International Version, Galatians 5:22-23a). As you might have seen with my giftings, not all giftings are the same as these fruits mentioned, but all such provisions are for the health and betterment of the Body, His church.

He desires to teach us how to allow Him to bring these forth. Thankfully, it is not hard work to bring these forth. They are gifts. There is no pain or pushing as with childbirth. They come forth naturally as we connect with the Holy Spirit and allow Him to lead us in our daily living. He teaches us how to walk this out.

Not only does this good Father provide gifts and fruit for His children, He also provides them with blessings beyond description. Shelter, food, clothing, funds, jobs, and all such blessings come from Him. He provides them, or helps us, to obtain them, and teaches us to accept and steward them.

God LOVES to bless His children with good things.

He loves to provide. He loves watching us use His gifts and provision. As we accept and steward them well, sharing them and using them for the Kingdom, He continues to pour more out to us, lavishing us with His goodness.

With Abraham, God displays His goodness as noted in Genesis, saying, "I will make you a great nation; I will bless you and make your name great; and you shall be a blessing. I will bless those who bless you, and I will curse him who curses you; and in you all the families of the earth shall be blessed." (New King James, Genesis 12:2-3)

Again, with Moses, God promises: *"...blessing I will bless you, and multiplying I will multiply your descendants as the stars of heaven and as the sand which is on the seashore; and your descendants shall possess the gate of their enemies. In your seed all the nations of the earth shall be blessed, because you have obeyed My voice."* (New King James, Genesis 22:17-18)

Then in Exodus, God declares a blessing, noting, *"So you shall serve the LORD your God, and He will bless your bread and your water. And I will take sickness away from the midst of you."* (New King James, Exodus 23:25) These are the kinds of blessings He loves to pour out on His children.

It's His joy to do so.

Those who are promised favor are then led to accept these blessings and carry out God's plans. The Lord gives them what is needed when they and others need it. He blesses His children as an example to the unsaved and as provision to the saved.

God's children are set apart for the work of His Kingdom.

We are set apart and holy. God calls us priests.[61] Priests are set apart for worship, to enjoy and celebrate the Lord. We connect, honor, and have fellowship with our Father, the King.

We, as priests, are responsible to care and intercede for the rest of the Body. God's children are to announce His holiness and convey the stories of His goodness and favor; we're to tell of the good news.

God wants to equip the Church to be a walking testimony of God's love and blessings, as well as signs of the need for repentance, forgiveness, and His perfect righteous judgment. Priests were once secluded in the temple. Now we, as priests are the temples and resemble the Holy of Holies, filled with the Holy Spirit. We are not hidden, but seen. We are to be the Lord's hands and feet as we share His will. Our

---

[61] 1 Peter 2:9

jobs include helping the needy, healing the sick, raising the dead, and casting out demons. We are to bring revival and call the masses to trust in and glorify the King. We are also to take the land back from the enemy.

This commission at times seems daunting, but the Lord teaches and equips us with the gifts, strength, and understanding to fulfill our callings.

He gave us His Word and His Spirit, our tutor and rabbi, who comforts the weary with His love, teaching us to do the same for others. He pours out waves of fresh faith and fresh fire, and in the process, heals us from old wounds and battle scars. Our battles aren't harmless, but we overcome and get back up in His strength.

As we grow in trust and experience, we can then turn around and help those around us by teaching them and equipping them for victory. We can learn compassion for others, that leads to action, so we in turn can help and heal the broken-hearted.

Furthermore, in our joy, trust, and freedom, we can serve our King by setting captives free—free to reign in the Kingdom in victory.

Setting the captives free and equipping the saints is our goal because it is His goal. [62]

He will accomplish His goals through us.

---

[62] Isaiah 61:1-2

Study Questions

1. He considers us worthy of His care, attention, and love, as noted in Isaiah 43:4. Does that feel true or are there reasons you feel unworthy of these things?

2. Read 1 Corinthians 12:4-11. What gift have you seen present in your own life?

3. Not all giftings are the same as these fruits mentioned. What other gift have you used in your life to be a blessing?

4. In what ways might the Lord be leading you to use these gifts?

12
Freedom for the Bride

In the Kingdom of God, there is one thing that is often quite different from the fairy tale stories we loved as kids. Like in the stories, there is a wedding and happily ever-after ending for the Bride; there is also a villain, a curse, and a rescuing prince. Unlike the stories, this Bride is the Body of Christ who came from a cursed world and once lived a sinful life.

This Bride isn't so pretty. She comes to the story war torn, weary, and bedraggled. She is also to blame. Legally, she needs pardon, and thankfully, this is done through the blood payment of the Lamb.

In the spirit world, all charges against her are now moot. The debt was paid in heaven's court by Jesus' blood. The Bride is legally determined to be spotless; however, the enemy continues to bring before the Judge a long list of other complaints against the Bride. These charges pertain to strongholds and agreements made with Satan. If there is a claim that He can bring forth because of an agreement or stronghold the Bride made with him, He will argue his right to access the Bride. He wants to maintain these agreements and strongholds.

These agreements are like tethers or chains that remain even after the blood payment for sin was applied.

When I was a new believer, I had strongholds and

agreements I had made with the enemy. There was a clean-up process needed because I was still a mess. My life was a mess. I had the enemy's fingerprints all over me. I needed to be set free from agreements I had made with Satan. I needed strongholds to be broken.

I may have been accepted into the King's courts as a mess, but there was a process of learning, healing, change, and freedom that still needed to take place.

As a new believer, I was unaware that I needed lots of cleaning up. There were many areas of my life and behaviors that needed to change. For example, my vocabulary was in need of cleansing. Thankfully, I had invited two Christians to be my roommates. One roommate felt led early on by the Lord to correct my choice of words. It was a habit she knew needed to be broken, and she called me on it. At the time, I thought my language was no big deal, but now, I rarely say those things and repent if I do.

This was a process of uncovering old ways of thinking and then changing because of a desire to line up my walk to the Word. There were more habits that needed to be cleaned up, but in the midst of that, I was led by the Holy Spirit to realize Satan still had claims on me because of agreements and strongholds I had made with him. I had been unaware of these. For example, I had made agreements with the spirit of fear and allowed him to remain as a false protector. At some point, I believed fear kept me safe. It was a stronghold or wall between me and the Lord. A stronghold of fear had to be broken so that I could be free.

Strongholds connect us to the enemy and allow him a way to hinder us.

Fixing these takes time, and the Lord is patient and

gracious, yet ties to the enemy still need to be broken. Though God is as merciful to us as Hosea was to his bride, He doesn't want to share His Bride with another!

Let me be clear: deliverance is not needed for the wedding. The blood and vow to be His were enough, but to be free to reign effectively by Christ's side in the Kingdom, deliverance is essential.

As long as we partner with the enemy and act out his will, even ignorantly, we are hindering the plans of the King and our relationship with Him.

This is why we have the Holy Spirit as a teacher, helper, and tutor for the Bride. The Holy Spirit is the true rabbi and teacher. Our Rabbi is a wise and gentle teacher, even when we are stubborn. The Holy Spirit helps us learn of the claims the enemy has against us and then helps us change in mind, agreement, and behavior.

There is a process of deliverance and purification wherein we must humble ourselves under the teaching and correction of the Holy Spirit. We are to throw off all that hinders us. The pride, selfishness, and rebellion we learned from the world and its king must be burned away, choice after choice, submission after submission.

His Bride is to be cleansed.

Ask the Lord what agreements you have made with the enemy. Consider how you may have partnered with and trusted him instead of God. As God shows you, cancel the agreements made and rebuke the enemy, sending him away.

If you feel unsure about this process, resources such as *Pigs in the Parlor* by Frank Hammond and *The Power of the Blood* by H.A. Maxwell Whyte are great helps!

Pray about these things. The Good Rabbi, the Holy Spirit will teach us the truth, cleanse and heal us, and also set us free. It is why He had to come and why Jesus had to go. [63]

We need Him.

We all need Him.

The enemy is a liar, and he works hard to maintain his connections to the Bride. He is such a proficient liar; even believers at times heed his voice.

We as brothers and sisters, are to claim this freedom and deliverance for ourselves and each other. We, as children and priests, are to proclaim freedom and release to those who are oppressed.

God wants every captive child freed and restored.

Sometimes, God intervenes and miraculously frees His children instantly. Often, however, it is a gentle process, and His children are supposed to help each other. This is why the Lord teaches and even commands His disciples to rebuke the devil and cast Him out.[64] Even recently, I personally needed such freedom when I had been saved for over twenty years. For me, I experienced a big change, and I felt the difference, but prior to the recent experience I had with deliverance, it had felt very slow going. I wrote earlier about the attack on our minds and the need we have to take every thought captive, but what happens when we fail to do so? Every person is a target for the enemy. Scripture notes that the devil is prowling like a hungry lion looking for his meal.[65] We may

---

[63] John 16:7

[64] James 4:7

[65] 1 Peter 5:8

be that meal if we are not on guard.

Each decision that compromises our righteousness, accepts what is unholy, or agrees with Satan, opens a door in the spiritual realm for him to gain access to us.

Through such a door, the enemy can enter, and lay claim to and harass the children of God (pre- and post-salvation). What are examples of these doors? They can be as simple as entertaining oneself with unclean media, walking in selfishness and unforgiveness, or agreeing with declarations that do not line up with Kingdom truths. Negative self-talk or negative words about others can cause false beliefs, separating God's children from the truth and creating strongholds for the enemy.

A stronghold is a battle term that depicts a fortified barrier or wall that protects from attack. The problem is that these strongholds are not built up against the enemy but set up against the King because of our own false beliefs, and agreements, fears, and doubts.

Fear is one of the biggest and most powerful strongholds. Fear is tricky as it portrays itself as a comfort, a wise guide or protector, and a buffer from harm. Instead, it hinders the relationship between child and Father. Just as with Adam and Eve, fear causes division. When we, as children, agree with fear instead of trusting God, a stronghold of the enemy is established.

This stronghold is strengthened with each agreement. After a while, it just seems like the new normal. The captive has been lulled into agreement and submission, unbeknownst to them.

We, as priests and princes (or princesses), are to help each other attain freedom from any and all agreements and to demolish or pull down strongholds.[66]

I will lend my own most recent example, as I noted earlier.

Since age thirteen, I have been a believer, and I have been truly walking with the Lord since my early twenties. Even so, throughout my walk, there had been an agreement with fear, as if it kept me safe. It was mild, but cumulative. Fear of harm, loss, and being out of control were lingering in the back of my mind and led me in countless decisions.

I had fought fear myself and through Christian counseling (as a licensed counselor, I knew of many interventions). I had rebuked my fears. I received prayer. Others had also rebuked fear and cast it out, pleading the blood over me. I had studied and taken classes on fear in seminary and beyond. I delivered others from fear and taught people how to do so, but fear *still* remained a companion.

Maintaining fear built a relationship with the enemy and caused me to make decisions based on his leadership.

I had fear in my life and therefore, made fear-based decisions since my early years, so I had no recollection of my decision to do so. The thoughts that aligned with fear were also passed down from previous generations and reinforced in society, so they seemed normal. So many voices, including my parents', were pleading that I be safe, be careful, agree with a spirit of fear and follow its lead.

Was I hearing voices? No. I am not referring to hearing *voices* as in clinical terms (though that is of the enemy as well). It is not an audible voice that speaks or leads. That might make picking up on the enemy easier, but no, these voices are

---

[66] 2 Corinthians 10:3-5

either messages from others led by the enemy (family, friends, teachers, or media) or a spiritual voice (or voices). These voices might seem like muffled chatter or white noise in the background. Generally, this later type is not easily perceived. The spirit of a believer will sometimes pick up on the communication from the enemy, almost as if the Lord opens the hearer's ears to the spirit realm.

The enemy generally likes to speak in first person, so that makes discerning him more difficult.

It was a long time until I became aware of how much of an impact fear really had on my life. I could not even see the depth or breadth of the stronghold(s) or his affect on my life until I was set free. For me, it was the Corona virus that brought these strongholds to the surface, as it probably has for many. Fear has been overtaking the thoughts of many people. I was one.

Instead of standing on the word of God for His rescue and protection (though I was praying, reading, and declaring His truth), I was still scouring the internet for information about the potential impact of Covid-19 and the 101 ways to avoid it. I wanted to hide. The rules made it easy to do so because we were told to stay home and avoid everyone. I liked this, or I was led to believe I did, because there I could control and maintain my own environment, setting up my kingdom with strongholds. But they weren't God's strongholds.

The false protections were suggested to me by the enemy, either directly or indirectly. I had allowed the enemy to build, or help me build, walls between myself and my protector, the King.

One day I was on a group call with co-elders of my

church. We were navigating the options for reopening our gatherings. There were rules and regulations to assist everyone to maintain health. I was all about these. I actually desired the church to remain closed so I could keep my kids and my family at home. I was communicating with the team and asked questions about safety, safety, safety.

Finally, my pastor had had enough! After ending the large group meeting, he asked me to stay on the chat and then proceeded to call out the spirit of fear, rebuke it, and lead me in deliverance with his wife and my husband in agreement.

He led me to consider with the Lord the memories in which I might have agreed with fear or wherein I was led strongly to agree with my need to be in control. I was reminded by the Lord of a time when I was four or five years old. I had pneumonia, so severely that I had to be hospitalized. I recalled that I was in a bed under an oxygen tent, and I was in need of an IV. Because I refused, my father held my arm for the nurse. I was afraid and felt betrayed.

At that moment, I was led by the enemy to believe that even my father couldn't be trusted. It was not true, but I was a child, and the enemy used this false interpretation to start a stronghold of fear in me.

My father had not betrayed me. He likely hated everything about that experience as much as I did, but this opened a door to fear and control that held on and grew for decades. The event impacted my trust in my heavenly Father. It impacted a myriad of interactions with the world and decisions made. It became a part of who I was, or so I thought.

However, it *wasn't* me.

I needed to be set free. Only then could I walk out my deliverance and freedom.

After that night of prayer and deliverance with my pastor, things seemed so starkly different. I seemed different to myself and to others. I seemed more childlike, less controlling. Humble. I was told I was glowing.

Inside and around me, things seemed airy, empty, and incredibly quiet. The ambient noise of demonic voices was gone. Their presence had left.

I had never experienced anything like it. Though I had tried to be free on my own, I needed help. I needed someone willing to take authority and action to set me free of what I had been unable to be free of. My pastor, his wife, and my husband, God's children, took on the enemy with authority and power when I could not.

God wants us all to gain awareness of the devil's schemes and of the truth of God's love, our authority, and gain victory over them.

We need to understand this so that we can pull down the strongholds in the spirit and demolish them for the King. We can come out of agreement with the enemy and take back what belongs to us and God. Then we can declare and seize freedom for ourselves and those who have been unable to.

I encourage you to consider any struggles you have had—any freedom you see someone else lacking. Prayerfully consider either seeking deliverance or graciously offering to assist others in need as they are willing.

You might need more than one believer to make the enemy take flight, but freedom is worth the fight.

Study Questions

1. What strongholds, as described in 2 Corinthians 10:3-4, and agreements might you have made with the enemy giving him a foothold, as in Ephesians 4:27?

2. In what ways have you made decisions based on the leadership of the enemy?

3. In what areas might you need to be set free and then walk out your deliverance?

4. Maybe take some time to come out of agreement with the enemy and realign your trust in the Lord as your hope and helper instead of the spirits who had previously led you.

Optional Prayer

"Lord, I repent of allowing _____ to lead and guide me, to have any power or authority over my life. I ask you to forgive me for letting another spirit other than yours lead, guide, help, and protect me. I was wrong. You are my Lord, my God, in whom I trust. I am coming out of agreement with that spirit now. Lord, in Your authority and name, I command that spirit of _____ to be bound and to go in Jesus' name!"

"Spirit of _____, Go in Jesus' powerful name! I am paid for by the blood of Christ. It covers all my sins and frees me from every agreement, so all your authority over me and my life is moot right now. Spirit of _____, no longer speak to me. Lord, please fill the spaces and roles that spirit took up. Be my guide, my stronghold, and my Lord in all things. I choose to come under your authority, leadership, and safety alone. Holy Spirit, please fill me. May my body only be used and led by you. May my mind be filled with your thoughts and not led or influenced by any other powers or spirits."

13
Walking It Out

How does a believer take this authority and put it into practice?

Jesus tells us in John 14:12 that we will do what He did and more. So then, what He did, we can do.

Let's examine what He did. Jesus changed water into wine. This was what He chose (or His mother chose) to do first. Now, I have yet to see or hear of someone doing this miracle, but if He said we can, I guess that is possible. No one really knows why He felt the need to do such a miracle in the circumstances. He did. Some speculate that perhaps Jesus did so in order to honor His mother. Maybe He didn't want the wedding hosts to be shamed. Either way, He did it, so we could, if need be.

He let this be His first miracle, Jesus' baseline. Scientifically, this miracle was to change the molecular structure of water into that of wine. No, I don't understand it, but maybe we don't have to understand. He asks us to have faith and be obedient, serving others as He leads.

He healed an official's son.

This was Jesus' second miracle. Now, there are two things that I contemplated when considering this miracle. First, this man was a Gentile. Therefore, this included more than "His people" and led to an openness to love beyond just the royal family of the Jewish people. It denoted compassion for the "others." In this, He leads us to do the same. We are to heal the broken with no respect for their heritage or who they are. After all, He is no *"respecter of persons."* (New International Version, Romans 2:11-16) Second, He had just said something very important before performing the miracle! This was, *"Unless you people see signs and wonders,"* Jesus told him, *"You will never believe."* (New International Version, John 4:48) Then He healed the boy anyway. This wasn't Him putting up a wall, but a declaration of truth. We are to heal, in part, because it will help others believe.

This miracle shows us we can heal the sick. He wants us to. Furthermore, not only did He heal the boy, but He did so at a distance. This means we can, too.

Can we heal all sickness, disease, and disfigurement? Well, we are told we don't even have a record of all the miracles Jesus did, but we do know many. The retained examples are enough to show us we can heal the blind, deaf, dumb, and paralyzed.

That is a substantial list even thus far, but in addition, He healed at least one leper, a man with dropsy (likely Parkinson's), a woman's chronic bleeding, and a severed ear.[67] Even if we did *these* things, it would substantially change our world and the testimony of God's goodness!

Again, if He did these things and said we can do all He did in His name, we can. Like Him, we can *"lay hands on the sick and they will recover."* (New King James, Mark 16:18)

What else did He show us how to do?

He fed countless people.

---

[67] Community in Mission. "37 Miracles of Jesus in Chronological Order". PDF. blog.adw.org. http://blog.adw.org/wp-content/uploads/2018/03/37-Miracles-of-Jesus-in-Chronological-Order.pdf, September 8, 2020

We are given numbers as to those present when he fed the masses, but the numbers never include women and children and there were more unaccounted-for miracles.[68] These provisions were not just purchased because He had money and bought food or caught because Jesus was really good at fishing (though He proved He knew how to make a great catch).[69] As with His first miracle, this was also miraculous!

Jesus manipulated what He had into what He did not have as He multiplied the fish and bread.

How might we help the hungry in this world if we did what he did?

I have yet to manufacture or cause food to materialize, but He showed us we can. In fact, He asked us to when He told us to do what He did. Furthermore, what He said to the disciples was, *"You give them something to eat."* (New International Version, Mathew 14:16)

We are to heal the sick and feed the hungry.

What else?

Jesus walked on water!

I certainly have not done this; however, if need be, I am sure He would help me to do so like Peter.[70] In fact, He displayed authority over water both by walking on it[71] and by speaking to it, as noted in Matthew 8:23-27.

---

[68] Matthew 14:13-21 and 15:32-39 (see also in Mark, Luke and John)

[69] Luke 5:1-11

[70] Matthew 14:29

[71] Matthew 14:22-33

If He portrayed for us an example of having authority over water in this way, then what else might we do with water in His name, given it is in His will?

Might we command storms to cease, change directions, or be quiet?

Maybe.

The waters were parted four times. It happened first during the exodus from Egypt when Moses lifted his rod;[72] again with Joshua at the entrance to the Promised Land[73] when the feet of those who carried the ark touched the water; also, with Elijah as he led the people over the Jordan;[74] and once more with Elisha as he struck the water.[75]

Each time, this was done when His chosen servants were obedient and partnered with the LORD.

Both my husband and my daughter have separate stories of believing for and declaring good weather when the skies predicted rain, only to enjoy the sun. Both donned their swimwear expectantly and rejoiced.

What other miracles was Jesus noted for?

Jesus cast out demons—lots of demons.

Surely, since He modeled this so strongly and taught the disciples to do the same, it must have been important.

Jesus modeled for us how to take authority over the devil and free those hindered by him and his demons. Sometimes,

---

[72] Exodus 14:15-22

[73] Joshua 3:5-17 through 4:1-18

[74] 2 Kings 2:8

[75] 2 Kings 2:12-15

Jesus didn't even *command* demons to leave! They *knew* His authority, and some even bartered with Him for their judgment before being cast into the swine and then the lake. [76]

We can walk in His name and character, doing the same for Him now.

Please note that acting out God's will in doing miracles is not to be done in a cocky, entitled manner, as it is not about the self. Such miracles are to be done with a humble surety of status in His Kingdom.

It is not in *our* authority alone that we can do this; it is in our authority *because* of Jesus' blood. Actually, He does the miracles for and through us, as noted in John 15:7-8, where Jesus said, *"If you abide in me, and my words abide in you, ask whatever you wish, and it will be done for you. By this my Father is glorified, that you bear much fruit and so prove to be my disciples."* (English Standard Version)

It is not for our own glory, but His!

Certainly, there are more miracles Jesus did, but let's focus on what might lead us to struggle with faith the most.

He raised people from the dead.[77]

In fact, God the Father and the Holy Spirit raised Jesus from the dead![78] That is mind-altering!

No, I have not raised anyone from the dead yet, but I say yet because He said we can do the things He did, and He raised the dead. I have heard many testimonies from others in the Kingdom who are out raising the dead. It is happening!

[76] Matthew 8:28-33, NIV

[77] John 11:1-45 and Matthew 9:18, 23-26

[78] Matthew 28

We should be earnest in our service to the Lord if such a situation arises in our midst. The Lord may desire the dead we see before us to be raised and raise them through us.

What about declaring and decreeing a thing?

Though I did find scripture in Job 22:28 noting this is true, most of the precedent for this seems to come by the actions of the Father, whom we are to act like. If He is raising us up to rule and reign in His Kingdom like He did.

We then can deduce, by Jesus' example, that we have the capability to follow in His footsteps and therefore decree things and rightly expect them to happen.

This is just some of what Jesus displayed and taught. He even said, *"Everything is possible for one that believes."* (New International Version, Mark 9:23) Everything. The word everything is a *big* word, isn't it?

When we believe and walk in our authority and abilities in the Spirit, we can do everything.

Everything!

If Jesus can only do what He sees the Father doing, might we also do what we see our LORD doing?

Can we attempt to believe such teachings from the mouth of our Savior? Did He portray enough authority and trustworthiness to make such wild statements valid?

What if we decided to not only trust Jesus, the Son of God, for our salvation, but also for our authority?

This is what He is calling us to now. These things and more!

As Paul writes, *"Let us cast off"* (English Standard Version, Roman's 3:4) everything that hinders us as we walk in authority with His Sword in our mouths as we take the land and set people free for our King!

Study Questions

1. After reading Mark 16:17-18, Acts 2:43, and Hebrews 2:4, what signs and wonders have you seen or experienced that strengthened your belief?

2. Read Mark 4: 35-41. Might we command storms to cease, change directions, or be quiet?

3. If we have the capability to follow in His footsteps, as noted in Matthew 4:19 and Matthew 28:18-20, what should we expect as we do?

4. Ask the Lord how you can follow His leadership and do what He did, as well as future opportunities to do so.

14
Ten Steps to Walking in Authority

This is the chapter you've been waiting for. We all want to know *how* to put this into practice and have miracles happen. Everyone wants ten steps, so here we...

1. Go!

Our first step is choosing to take up our Kingdom authority and use it outside our homes, or at least outside ourselves. Jesus didn't model serving Himself. He modeled serving others. In order to serve others, we have to be *with* others. In fact, we have to be with others who are in need. These are the broken, the homeless, the hungry, the sick, and the needy.

We are to go wherever God leads us with feet outfitted with the Gospel, ready to share the good news, which includes health and freedom. We are to go help the Lord fulfill *His* will and bring His Kingdom of heaven to earth. His will might be in places we would rather not go. Maybe it's the prison or the homeless center; perhaps the courthouse or the gas station on the corner. The Lord will lead, but are we willing to follow?

I once felt very strongly that I needed to go to the mall. Now, I certainly don't mind shopping, but this was not about shopping. He was leading me to go. I went and wandered around, wondering why I was supposed to be there. At one point, I went into a shoe store. There, I felt led to ask if I could pray for the saleswoman who happened to be alone in the store. When I asked, she lit up, but she was also near tears. Her mother was to have open heart surgery the next day! She was so moved by my request to pray. It was just what she needed. The Lord knew her heart, which moved Him to action. I was the willing messenger.

God has called us to "go," and sometimes we pray, feed the hungry, or heal the sick.

Of course, before we go, we should fill such needs in our own homes. We are not to neglect this. In fact, we are to do so first,[79] but then we should go out and serve others outside our homes, outside our churches, and outside our comfort zones.

As we go, we need direction. Not only do we need to know where to go, we also need to know who to serve and with what. To do this, we must...

2. Listen!

God wants you to carry out His will and for things to happen, but remember, it is about His will. We have to get out with others to carry out His will, but we are not to just go make whatever we think is best happen. In order to go to the right place and carry out His will, we need to understand His will for the day, time, or situation. Each situation and need is different.

We cannot follow an exact formula and have the same result each time. That isn't how the Kingdom works. Why? For one reason, each situation is different. Each person is different.

---

[79] 1 Timothy 5:8

Each time we step out in faith and authority, the process will be different. We need to be listening and open to the leading of the Holy Spirit so we can do as He asks and desires.

Only God understands the current needs of a person, their history and hurts, as well as their needs for the future. I may think every deaf person needs to be able to hear right now, but what if that result at that exact time would not bless the person? We have no idea how changes will play out in the future, so we must allow God's will and not demand our own plan when we exercise authority, no matter what the situation.

When I became a Christian, I started attending a non-charismatic Southern Baptist church. Soon after, when I met my husband, I attended a very charismatic church with him occasionally. At that church, people fell down in the Spirit. I didn't understand. I didn't agree, and, in many ways, I judged them as being misled or even just wanting attention.

At some point, a few years later, I attended a conference at another church. It was a charismatic church as well. After the pastor gave his message, he was laying hands on people and praying for them. I was all for the prayer, but some people were falling down. I still did not understand this, and I was uncomfortable with it, but I had often asked God about it.

That day, the pastor came and prayed for me, but instead of laying hands on me, he stood there and blew on me.

I fell back to the floor! I laughed all the way down and continued to while I was on the floor. God knew and probably told the pastor that if he touched me, I would fight him and refuse to go down. That would have been true. So, instead, he listened, obeyed, and blew me over. I am so thankful that this brother in Christ was willing to do what seemed kind of ridiculous in the flesh but was perfect in the Spirit. God knew what I needed.

God knows what everyone and each situation needs.

Every person and situation will be different. It is crucial that we see what the Father is doing. We must be listening, studying, and waiting on Him to show us what each situation requires. Sure, we can lay hands on everyone who is sick and pray, but the person in front of us might need us to...

3. Have faith!

As we interact with people and listen, we will be led to act. We need faith to go and be willing to do what He has called us to do, without fear of what might happen. The pastor that blew on me was willing to follow the leading of a wise God and carry out His plans, even at the risk of looking silly or offending others. We choose to have faith in the wisdom of God and trust His plans and timing.

We need information and power because we are not the Healer; the Spirit is, so it is His job to carry it out. We are to be like a pipe tipped in the right direction.[80] It is the Holy Spirit who flows out and does what is needed.

Once, my daughter decided to test God's willingness and ability to provide food miraculously. So, she brought a pot to the potluck—an empty one. Unfortunately, we forgot it in the car, but when we got home and she remembered, she brought it outside and, while in the driveway, prayed over it. She prayed and waited for it to be filled with our evening meal.

We brought the pot inside after a while. She wasn't upset. It was still empty, but we were still believing and

---

[80] Dematos, Lee. Pastor. Sermon. Indian Lake Church. 2019. Worcester, MA

waiting. Just after we came in, a neighbor knocked on the door. He had a large pizza in his hand and offered it to us! Not only was this completely shocking to us, but it was also even more of a miracle because his son was having a teenage birthday with lots of teenage boys! How would they have extra? It was God! God knew my daughter would love pizza! She also loves people, so she saw a guest AND got a surprise pizza! God knew what would bless her more.

Each prayer is for a unique person with specific needs, wants, and desires. They have situations and histories we cannot possibly know. God does. We are not required to understand, but to go with a flexible and willing spirit.

Should we pray for someone who is deaf to hear? Yes! We should expect the hearing to come as well, but still...

4. Be flexible.

We need to be flexible regarding how, what, and when to pray. Consider Jesus' prayers. None of them were the same. Sometimes he used mud, other times He laid hands on people, but still other times He was far from the person He prayed for, and they still were healed.

What about the prideful commander, Naaman, in 2 Kings? Naaman wanted Elisha to come out and heal him, but instead the prophet's servant directed him to the dirty and murky Jordan River. The man was only healed when he finally agreed to dunk himself seven times. Elisha was led to pray in a different way, but he had the right result. Naaman was cured of pride and leprosy because of his willingness to agree to the process. He needed to...

5. Trust the Lord.

As we press in to hear the Lord's leading, He will show us how to pray, even if we should lay hands on someone or instead command something to leave. Sometimes symptoms are from a spirit and not an injury. If this is true, the Lord is likely to lead the one praying to inquire about the person's past and discover strongholds and agreements made with unclean spirits (demons).

The one praying can inquire if the person wishes for the spirit to be cast out and can do so. We have authority to rebuke spirits of darkness and command them to leave and let people go, but if the person does not want the spirit to go, that spirit has the right to remain. Generally, one would not rebuke a spirit in this case. Surprisingly, if someone does not want to change, it might be better to leave them as they are.

God's word notes, *"When an impure spirit comes out of a person, it goes through arid places seeking rest and does not find it. Then it says, 'I will return to the house I left.' When it arrives, it finds the house unoccupied, swept clean and put in order. Then it goes and takes with it seven other spirits more wicked than itself, and they go in and live there. And the final condition of that person is worse than the first. That is how it will be with this wicked generation."* (New International Version, Matthew 12:43-45) This isn't always the case, but we must rely on God's Word and the Spirit's leading in each situation, trusting He knows best. God knows what we need, and He has provided it. It is up to us to be willing.

6. Bring the Good News!

We cannot be so focused on physical needs that we neglect the soul. People need salvation!

Sometimes people need our focus and time to be more about their faith in the Healer than the healing. It is crucial that this fact is not overlooked. Healing a broken leg, but missing the soul removes an opportunity for salvation.

Moreover, even if someone has accepted Jesus as their Savior, they still might need realignment in their spiritual connection with the Lord. Maybe they are more aware of their sin than their salvation and need to be reminded of His love and...

7. Forgive

Forgiveness is the foundation of why Jesus came and died. For the freedom Christ paid for to be given and received, not only must we receive forgiveness and forgive others, but we are also to assist others to forgive and be forgiven. Our authority includes binding and loosing, for His word says, *"Truly I tell you, whatever you bind on earth will be bound in heaven, and whatever you loose on earth will be loosed in heaven." (New International Version, Matthew 18:18)* He even added the *"Truly I tell you,"* He confirmed our right to do so!

What does this mean to bind or loose?

Binding and loosing are legal terms. What the church, His Body, deems good or sinful is ratified as such in heaven. Each member of the church can release forgiveness or excommunicate others. *"Whether the verdict was the excommunication of the offender* ("bind") *or his pardon and restoration* ("loose"), *the ratification of the apostles was required, and would be made good in heaven."*[81] Jesus spoke of this saying, *"If you forgive anyone's sins, their sins are forgiven; if you do not forgive them, they are not forgiven."* (New International Version, John 20:22-23, parenthesis mine) That is powerful!

The world needs forgiveness. The Body needs forgiveness. Might it be that we speak for the LORD to release

---

[81] "Matthew 18:18." Matthew 18:18 Commentaries: "Truly I Say to You, Whatever You Bind on Earth Shall Have Been Bound in Heaven; and Whatever You Loose on Earth Shall Have Been Loosed in Heaven., Pulpit Commentary., Bible Hub, 2004, biblehub.com/commentaries/matthew/18-18.htm. 2, August, 2020

it? We need each other for this. We must help each other and…

8. Partner.

Sometimes we are to go alone, but having backup is also important! Warfare is active and all around us. Alone, we have a greater risk of being sidetracked, hindered, or harmed by the enemy. Having a prayer covering or a team can build strength and protection. Ecclesiastes 4 notes, *"Though one may be overpowered, two can defend themselves."* (New International Version, Ecclesiastes 4:12) Perhaps this is why Jesus often sent the disciples out in pairs. Were they not more effective?

As you prepare to go and walk out your authority, ask at least one other person to keep you in prayer. Of course, it is also essential to partner with the Holy Spirit. He will be the one to teach and lead you, and then you can…

9. Teach

As Jesus teaches, he also teaches His students to teach.

Take someone with you as you go. Come alongside someone as they go to help them learn, understand, and walk in their redeemed role in the Kingdom. Encourage them in their faith. Exercise grace as you help those who are trying to do what you have done, so they do it better than you! Rejoice with them when they do, and help them remember the truth when they struggle against the enemy or doubt.

Partner with others and pray for them continually, reaching out on purpose to check in with them. Everyone has hard days and times when they need help.

We are told to go make disciples. This is not just helping others to know what Jesus did, but assisting them to *do* what Jesus did. This is part of our need to…

10. Take Responsibility

We have a responsibility to do the Lord's work. God has designed, destined, and decided to equip us with all we need for His assignments, but we are responsible for following through. We are responsible for the going and doing. If we are unwilling to go when He makes a way, that failure is on our hands.[82]

Consider the parable of the talents in Matthew. When the servant was afraid of the master, he hid the talent God gave him. The master was displeased answering, *"'You wicked, lazy servant! So you knew that I harvest where I have not sown and gather where I have not scattered seed? Well then, you should have put my money on deposit with the bankers, so that when I returned I would have received it back with interest. So take the bag of gold from him and give it to the one who has ten bags. For whoever has will be given more, and they will have an abundance. Whoever does not have, even what they have will be taken from them. And throw that worthless servant outside, into the darkness, where there will be weeping and gnashing of teeth.'"* (New International Version, Matthew 25:26-30)

The Lord is displeased when we withhold healing, freedom, or forgiveness from others to whom we could have released it. Every moment counts.

There is no shame for your past, but there is an urgency for action now. Each moment is a possible God encounter for someone—maybe you.

---

[82] Ezekiel 3:18

Study Questions

1. In what ways have you felt led to "Go," as noted in Matthew 28:19?

2. Read 2 Timothy 2:15 and 1 Samuel 3:1-10. How might you create a habit of listening, studying, and waiting on Him to show you?

3. Is there a church or group you might partner with to walk out what He is leading you to do?

4. How might the Lord be leading you to share and impact others with the Gospel through your gifts?

15
Not Alone

If you are overwhelmed, that is understandable. I am writing about doing miracles, overtaking the powers of darkness, and freeing humans from the enemy. It is overwhelming, and it would be too much for us to do alone. In fact, it would be impossible.

We cannot do this alone.

We aren't supposed to. This is why we are given the Holy Spirit. He is given to us because we need Him and because God believes we can do what He has asked *with* Him.

In order to accomplish anything for the Kingdom, we must be in a right relationship with the Lord. This requires time and attention to Him in prayer. Prayer is communication, but more listening than speaking. Yes, God wants a full relationship, but He already knows much of what we might tell Him. To serve well, we must listen well.

Good listening is both listening to the Holy Spirit and reading His Word. It means paying attention *as* we go and *before* we go. It is choosing to be quiet and lay down our plans in an effort to listen for His. It is tuning into the broadcast of His heart and desires for His beloved.

I used to think prayer was like an officer listening for commands or orders from the top, but truly, it is more like a waltz. We stay close, almost as one with the Lord, and let Him lead. We look at Him, not the floor or in the direction we are going. Our eyes are upon Him.

Moving with the Holy Spirit is like a dance.

The Holy Spirit wants us to partner with Him so He can help us at every turn and in every situation. Like the lead of a hand in a dance, His quiet promptings are all that is needed to lead us if we are attentive. We don't always (maybe not even usually) understand where He is leading, but as we follow, we learn and are equipped for what He leads us to.

As we follow the Lord, He will help us to mature from needing milk to devouring the meat of the scriptures. He helps us to understand the Bible and His heart. We need His help. He is our tutor.

Every Prince and Princess needs a tutor.

Jesus is our example of trusting the Holy Spirit as a tutor. Not only did Jesus show us how to partner with the LORD, but He also gave examples and taught us how to partner with each other. The Lord does not want us to go through life or fight alone. He began this example with Adam and Eve. They were to partner and help one another. God even mentioned that He created Eve because Adam could use some help.

God designed marriage as a union that makes each individual stronger when together. He generally puts two very different people together so that they each have strengths that help the other's weakness. The differences can cause struggles, but the struggles can bring refinement if allowed.

My husband and I are different in many ways. I am a bold, goal-oriented, choleric personality walking in prophetic gifts. I ponder the meaning of things, consider the big picture, and connect dots quickly so I can jump into action. He patiently brings the detail I miss and encourages me not to jump ahead. As a relaxed, phlegmatic worship leader with a gift of joy, my husband helps me laugh, slow down, and give the big picture back to God. We help, bless, and balance each other. We don't study the word, tackle problems, or even serve the Lord in the same way. We don't process information the same way either, but together, we partner well.

We are supposed to be part of a team.

This is not only why he created Eve, but also why he gave Aaron to Moses and gathered the twelve. He didn't make Moses go alone, and Jesus recruited twelve disciples to be a team. He walked with them, showing them all he was going to do. He showed them how to be like Him, and how to work with each other in the process.

I am sure these guys didn't just magically get along. Some of these were fishermen noted for quarrelling; there was also a scholar, two violent nationalists, and a tax collector.[83] It's likely they fought; in fact, two of the disciples (James and John) were called *"sons of thunder"*[84] who wanted to call down fire from heaven.[85] Jesus was likely the referee for them at least once. Like us, they came from different places, but were called to work together.

We are called to work together.

In unity, we help each other to walk in the victory we have in Jesus. We are called to go together because two are better than one.[86] God initiated teamwork and knew we

---

[83] Unknown. "Who Were the 12 Disciples?" *Bibleinfo.com*, Voice of Prophecy, 2020, www.bibleinfo.com/en/questions/who-were-twelve-disciples. 9.3.2020

[84] Mark 3:17

[85] Luke 9:54

[86] Ecclesiastes 4:9

would need to be different to be most effective, giving everyone gifts, and specifically, some to be *"apostles; and some, prophets; and some, evangelists; and some, pastors and teachers."* (New King James, Ephesians 4:11-13) All these can work together in the Kingdom. This is called the five-fold ministry. We are aligned to minister together with our giftings and callings, which usher in the fullness of the Kingdom.

Whether we are different in denominations, color, heritage, gender, or strengths, the differences are meant to fortify God's church and complete the "puzzle" that is the Body of Christ.

It is the unified Body of Christ partnering with the Holy Spirit that can overcome the world.

Study Questions

1. In John 14:26, John 16:13-14, and Acts 1:8, how is the Holy Spirit our helper or tutor? (If you have not asked the Holy Spirit to come dwell in you, now is a great time to do so!)

2. Partnering can be both helpful and hard. How have attempts at partnering worked with others or not worked as you have tried to serve Him? How have you been successful in working with others?

3. Are there any relationships where you might not be in unity? How might the Lord be leading you regarding those?

4. Read Ephesians 4:11-13 and look at the gifts or Kingdom roles listed. Jesus walked in all the gifts, and likewise, we can walk in them all at times. Which of these seems more like your gift or gifts?

16

His Children Teach

Go and make disciples.

Jesus makes it very clear that we have a Kingdom assignment to make disciples, to make His Kingdom bigger, and to go forth and, multiply as in Genesis.[87] Most often, multiplication is connected with the birthing of babies. However, Kingdom multiplication is also about bringing spiritual babies into the Kingdom and raising them up.

Part of our commission is to preach the gospel and help the lost, those outside the Kingdom, as they repent and become His children. Still, there is another aspect that is critical to maintenance and increase in the Kingdom: replication.

Jesus called His followers disciples. Disciples are to grow to be like their Teacher, Jesus. Notice I didn't say they were to be like their teachers. Our teachers are not to be replicated. Jesus is.

We are to teach in a way that points not to ourselves, but to our Brother Jesus, to the Father, and to the Holy Spirit as helpers with the goal of growing the Kingdom.

The King wants us to be one Body, the Church. No, we can't physically become one in the flesh. Believers could no more do this than be born again out of our mother's womb,

---

[87] Genesis 9:7

but we can be one flesh in our mindset, actions, and goals. We can, however, increase our attitude of repentance by turning from our own desires and aligning ourselves with God's. In this, we become one together in His likeness.

Discipleship is essential for believers as they clean and reprogram themselves from the world. We must walk together, holding each other up to the standard of the Most Holy One. We can become examples for others to learn from.

Will we, in this life, meet perfection in our flesh? No, but we press on toward perfection as we move heavenward in His grace[88] and we learn and grow more and more.

Then we make disciples.

We teach.

This means teaching the Scriptures, but another way to teach is to share testimonies. Testimonies teach volumes. I often share testimonies of how God helped, blessed, or changed me; He even corrected me in order to help others. I want people to learn from my mistakes, so they don't need to make the same ones I did.

There is no place for pride when testimonies are available.

There are times where I have taught others what I have just recently learned or experienced with the Lord. An example of a testimony I shared has to do with my own deliverance. After I experienced being set free, I soon told someone else what I had learned. We prayed and explored the struggles that person had, and in doing so, they were able to have a similar experience of healing and deliverance.

<u>I shared because the</u> Holy Spirit led me to; He loves

---
[88] Philippians 2:12-15

them, and I love them. We both want them to benefit. In love, believers must turn, and help others as their service to the Lord. This is part of the *"loving one another"* we are commanded to do. (New International Version, John 13:34-35) In loving a brother or sister, we help them move forward and grow.

Grace, timing, and prayer are necessities in sharing or teaching. For example, to just go and tell everyone we see that they need deliverance would not be loving or graceful! It might cause more harm than good. Listening for the prompting of the Holy Spirit and honoring His timing and methods is important.

With wisdom, believers either share or withhold a matter, waiting for the proper timing to speak. There is *"a time to be silent and a time to speak..."* (New International Version, Ecclesiastes 3:7b)

Timing is so important.

A closed-minded listener is not a learner.

We must begin with a trusting relationship and gain the ear of a listener for them to heed what we teach and share. We must do so in love. Furthermore, our guidance is accepted by hearers because of their need. People accept teaching because they have a recognized need and desire to apply what is learned.

Teaching must be both relevant and useful.

The Word of God is a double-edged sword, but only for those who take it up and handle it wisely, discerning its application. We are to show our brothers and sisters how to apply Biblical teaching(s). As we are led by the Lord, it might be appropriate to ask a brother or sister questions such as:

How do you read the Bible?

What does that verse mean?

How do you listen to the Spirit?

How do you know when and how to apply these Scriptural truths?

All these questions arise for us all as we walk with the Lord. The answers to questions like these often come from Bible study. As we learn from studying or from pastors and teachers who expound on the word, we gain understanding and can share the answers to these questions, helping each other. As their understanding grows, we can share more and more complex teachings, so they grow in faith and wisdom. Every believer starts with spiritual milk but then moves on to meat.[89]

The table is set for us all, but not everyone is ready to partake of everything on the table.

The health of the teacher is also important. We should not assume the role of the teacher when we are faltering. Still, it depends on to what degree we are struggling. Everyone is working out salvation with fear and trembling,[90] but the teacher should be in alignment with the true Rabbi.

In an emergency, a flight attendant teaches grownups to put masks on themselves before they attempt to put one on their child. This is because they themselves need to be alive and well to help their children. Likewise, we need to be well before providing help to others. I do not mean we have to be perfect theologians or pastors to teach. Certainly not! We

---

[89] 1 Corinthians 3:2a and Hebrews 5:13-14

[90] Philippians 2:12

should, however, be in a place of humility and in a right relationship with the Lord.

Once we receive a right standing with the Lord, we can teach and help others in recovery. To attempt to teach while faltering (or having fallen) ourselves is unhealthy and can certainly come across as hypocritical to the listener. Unhealthy teachers hinder God's message and can lead to false doctrines, but should we cease to teach because we are imperfect? Certainly not! We are all growing. Never assume you are too imperfect to teach, as God's grace is sufficient for us all[91]. We all struggle as we grow.

In the places where you stand, love others and help them up.

---

[91] 2 Corinthians 12:9

Study Questions

1. Read Matthew 28:19-20 and Acts 1:8. How can you walk in the Kingdom assignment to make disciples?

2. Testimonies are the stories of what God has done for us. These can be faith-building and prophetic, unlocking faith in others. Read Revelation 19:10. What testimonies do you have, or have you heard, that you could share to encourage or teach others?

1. In Psalm 23:5, the table is set with all we need. We are invited to be His guests. He sets before us a cup representing His blood, the provision we need as the payment for our sin and abundance for all our needs. The oil on the table represents sanctification and therefore freedom, in addition to the gifts of gladness and joy. Picture yourself at His table. Is there anything lacking as you sit with Him?

2. James 3:1 speaks to our need to be healthy before we teach others. After reading that verse, list and bring to the Lord any areas in your life that the Lord is leading you to tend to.

17
The Kingdom Is Love

"Little children, I am with you a little while longer. You shall seek Me; and as I said to the Jews, I now say to you also, 'Where I am going, you cannot come.' A new commandment I give to you, that you love one another, even as I have loved you, that you also love one another. "By this all men will know that you are My disciples, if you have love for one another." (New International Version, John 13:33-35)

The Kingdom is all about Love.

One of the more important things to be taught in this book or the Kingdom, is that we are to love one another. We are to care for the needs of one another, surrendering ourselves as living sacrifices.[92] We are to overtake the earth to care for it, and humanity.

Children of the King love one another. This "one another" refers both to those who are not yet children of God and those already in the Kingdom.

We in the Kingdom have been tasked with reigning in LOVE as the King would. In this way, His will is done, and His Kingdom comes. The Bible is filled with examples and references to God's care, and servanthood of others. God cared for Adam and Eve before and after the fall, even covering them with animal skins and sending them out. Noah and His family were cared for in the ark and with the ark

[92] Romans12:1b

itself. Later, Moses, Aaron, and Aaron's sons are directed to care for the people, as noted in Numbers, which reads, *"...before the tabernacle of meeting, were Moses, Aaron, and his sons, keeping charge of the sanctuary, to meet the needs of the children of Israel..."* (New King James, Numbers 3:38) They were to meet their needs and care for them.

God was showing them what was best and then leading them to do His will.

In the Old Testament, the family of God was divided into twelve groups of children. These were called the tribes. Within these, there was one tribe, the Levites, who were set apart for the care and service to God, and to the other eleven tribes (and women and children). As told, *"They may minister with their brethren in the tabernacle of meeting, to attend to needs..."* (New King James, Numbers 8:26)

The Levites were specifically assigned to care for the other tribes and the sanctuary, like our modern-day pastors are called to do.

Likewise, Jesus told His disciples to care for the sick, raise the dead and drive out demons as needed. He also had them practice feeding the hungry.[93] He reinforced the practice of caring for those in need. He even gave the needs of His mother to John at the cross, telling him, *"Here is your mother."* (New International Version, John 19:27)

He cares that we are cared for.

Later, in Acts after the resurrection, we find the believers *"were together, and had all things in common, and sold their possessions and goods, and divided them among all, as anyone had need. So continuing daily with one accord in the temple, and*

---

[93] Mark 6:37

breaking bread from house to house, they ate their food with gladness and simplicity of heart," (New International Version, Acts 2:46)

And we need not stop there for examples. In Romans, we can also read, *"Be kindly affectionate to one another with brotherly love, in honor giving preference to one another; not lagging in diligence, fervent in spirit, serving the Lord; rejoicing in hope, patient in tribulation, continuing steadfastly in prayer; distributing to the needs of the saints, given to hospitality."* (New King James, Romans 12:10-13)

This is Kingdom life.

This is the lifestyle we have been called to have as God's children.

The Kingdom is set up to have us bless each other.

In Acts 4:32-35, the Word depicts this. It reads, *"Now the multitude of those who believed were of one heart and one soul; neither did anyone say that any of the things he possessed was his own, but they had all things in common. And with great power the apostles gave witness to the resurrection of the Lord Jesus. And great grace was upon them all. Nor was there anyone among them who lacked; for all who were possessors of lands or houses sold them, and brought the proceeds of the things that were sold, and laid them at the apostles' feet; and they distributed to each as anyone had need."* (New King James, Acts 4:32-35)

The Kingdom of God sounds like a pretty good Kingdom set up by a good King, doesn't it? But keep in mind that the children of the Kingdom are the ones caretaking.

We are to reign with care.

We need to step into and fulfil the role He has called us to. We are to be God's hands and feet here on earth. We are to listen to the promptings of the Holy Spirit to hear what we personally are to do with our assets of time, money, and property. As we listen, in each moment, day, and year, whether at home, work, or in the streets, we will be led to love.

We are to love those we might deem unlovely.

God did not just ask us to love those who are easy to love. No! In fact, Jesus noted that even sinners do that. [94] Instead, we are to be rewarded when we love and do good to our enemies, when we give to those who cannot repay us. God would prefer we be like a "good" Samaritan instead of a Pharisee, that we tarry in love for another even when others deem it meaningless or beneath us.[95]

Such love was never beneath Christ.

Acting out love for one another is a priority in the Kingdom, for God is love. As His children, we must put on love each day by being His hands, feet, mouth, and heart in order that this love is displayed.

God wants His love to be made famous. We are the ones to make His name famous. With each act of kindness and care in His name, the world learns who He is.

The famous one.

The true and good King.

May He bring us into His chambers so that we may delight in Him.[96]

---

[94] Luke 6:32

[95] Luke 10:25-37

[96] Song of Solomon 1:4

Study Questions

1. The Bible has much to say about how we are to treat one another. Read Romans 12:10, 12:14, Philippians 2:3, and Ephesians 4:32. How are we taught to love one another?

2. Read Exodus 20:2-17. How is each of the ten Commandments an unction of love as fulfilled in John 13:34-35. How might you walk out love in your relationships?

3. We are to be God's hands and feet here on earth. Read Romans 10:15, 1 John 4:7-11, and 1 Peter 4:10-11. Is there someone you can choose to share love with tomorrow in a new way? What gifts and talents can you use to serve others?

4. Read Psalm 45:17 and Acts 20:24. We are to make His name famous. Might you still battle any fear of sharing His name with others, as Romans 1:16 leads us to do? Perhaps now is a good time to bring those areas to the Lord. What is He saying to you about any concerns you have?

18
Toss Your Crown

I hope to have added to your understanding of our call to reign for the King and our power and authority to do so by His Spirit. I hope to have encouraged you, my reader, to walk in God's authority and to put your crown on, accepting the call to go to battle and taking ground for your King. I do, however, want to be clear: there is also a time to toss your crown.

We mustn't neglect our crown when serving the King in this life as we advance His Kingdom. We shouldn't neglect it in battles against demons, angels, or principalities, for there we must stand in our authority, but to the King's feet we will also toss our crowns.

God alone is worthy of our complete praise, humility, and honor.

As much as we are worthy, able, and designed to reign with Him, the Lord is *much* more worthy to do so and to be honored for doing so. He in Himself is worthy, worthy of our humility and our understanding that we will never be King.

There is only one true King!

All those who wish to reign in the Kingdom must also celebrate the King, our God in all of His persons.

I have, in this text, written of Jesus as Brother, the Father as King, and the Holy Spirit as Tutor. Still, they are one. We are to worship and honor them all. If any of us do not do so, we are unworthy of His grace and residence in the Kingdom.

Though we have great worth because God deemed us worthy, next to Him, we pale in comparison. Because of His holiness, we must bow. We must put on humility, and we must toss our crowns at His feet. He is the I AM, the beginning and the end.

There is no Kingdom to be had without Him.

It is His.

We are His.

At the end of the day, the end of all days, we shall gladly toss our crowns at His feet and declare His worth.

I have not been blessed with an understanding of who the twenty-four elders[97] are who toss their crowns at His feet, but we are to do the same. For now, we can echo, *"Your will be done on earth as it is in heaven!"* (New King James, Matthew 6:10b) and we honor His Name, serving Him diligently, for He is coming soon...

Till that day, "Hold fast what you have, so that no one may seize your crown." (New International Version, Revelation 3:11)

---

[97] Revelation 4:10

Study Questions

1. Read 2 Timothy 2:12. Are you ready to reign with Him and accept your identity as a child of God and the call to go as His child into the world, taking ground as in Numbers 33:53, and go fishing for men (His lost children) as in Matthew 4:19?

2. How can you also celebrate the King, our God and Father in all His persons based on 1 Corinthians 10:31 and Romans 12:1?

3. Read Revelation 3:11. Satan is the fallen one who wants you to believe you can't wear your crown. How can you keep your crown on?

4. What have you learned about your place in the Kingdom and your identity as a child of God?

About the Author

Carrie Ann Barrette is a licensed mental health counselor and leader who has been counseling, writing, and speaking for nearly two decades. She earned a Master of Arts in Religion and a Master of Arts in Counseling from Gordon-Conwell Theological Seminary.

Carrie Ann delivers insights based on the Word of God, with practical steps, real-life stories, and spiritual discernment that will transform the way you think about and perceive the reality of God's kingdom.

Learn More About Carrie Ann Barrette

---

www.carrieannbarrette.com
www.liveoutlove.me
Facebook: https://www.facebook.com/CABarrette
Instagram: Carrieannbarrette
Twitter: CarrieABarrette

Live Out Love

Literature and Publishing

www.liveoutlove.me

Made in United States
North Haven, CT
03 January 2024